PICTORIAL HISTORY OF
MILITARY AIRCRAFT

PICTORIAL HISTORY OF
MILITARY
AIRCRAFT

Edited by John Pimlott

GALLERY BOOKS
An imprint of W.H. Smith Publishers Inc.
112 Madison Avenue
New York, New York 10016

A Bison Book

Published by Gallery Books
A Division of W H Smith
Publishers Inc.
112 Madison Avenue
New York, New York 10016

Produced by
Bison Books Corp.
15 Sherwood Place
Greenwich, CT 06830

ISBN 0-8317-6892-4

Printed in Hong Kong

1 2 3 4 5 6 7 8 9 10

PAGE 1: *Hans-Joachim Marseille,
nicknamed the 'African Eagle,'
poses in the cockpit of his
Messerschmitt Bf-109F-4 in North
Africa, March 1942.*

PAGES 2-3: *A Soviet MiG-29, NATO
codename 'Fulcrum,' shows its
lines. Designed as an air-
superiority fighter, the MiG-29
can take off from sections of road
close to the battlefront.*

THIS PAGE: *Short Stirling four-
engined night-bombers of the
RAF, photographed in 1944. By
then, they had been relegated to
the role of transports.*

CONTENTS

INTRODUCTION

The history of warfare in the twentieth century is inextricably linked to the history of air power and aircraft development. In 1900, as British forces fought their Boer enemies in South Africa, battles were still self-contained, two-dimensional affairs, involving groups of armed men restricted by their inability to see much beyond the contours of the ground. Some experiments had been conducted using lighter-than-air balloons for observation, but the advantages to be gained from such static, unwieldy equipment were limited. It was not until December 1903 when the Wright brothers made their epic flight in a heavier-than-air machine, that the first controllable and maneuverable aircraft emerged.

Although it took time for aircraft to be recognized as instruments of war, their impact was undeniable and, as World War I progressed, a number of basic roles – reconnaissance/observation, maintenance of airspace, naval support and bombing – were developed and refined. Their emergence extended the scope of war, adding a third dimension to battle and opening up the areas affected by the conflict. Nowhere was this more true than in the role of the bomber, for once the principle of dropping high explosives through the air had been accepted, any area within range of aircraft could constitute a target, even far behind the battlelines in the enemy homeland. Indeed, the concept of 'total war' in which combatants aim for the complete destruction of their enemies' political, social and economic systems, depended on the development of aircraft, for without the means of carrying out 'strategic bombing' of civilian and industrial areas, such destruction would have been impossible. In simple terms, aircraft ensured that no one was safe from the effects of war and that any distinction which may have previously existed between civilians and military personnel all but disappeared. The development and use of the air-delivered atomic bomb by August 1945 merely served to reinforce the point.

But the impact of combat aircraft has been much wider than that, adding new capabilities to forces on or near the battlefield which, as the century progressed, transformed the nature of war. Troops in the front-line became subject to air attack and were forced to defend themselves with ever more sophisticated anti-air weapons (a situation which produces a constantly swinging pendulum of advantage as aircraft and ground forces search for new methods of survival), while at the same time, the ability to move units around the battle area or from one battle area to another, using helicopters or long-range transports, added fresh mobility to the art of war. At sea, the situation was very similar, enhancing the ability of navies to maneuver for advantage, using information gained through the air, and to attack at longer range with increased accuracy using air-delivered weapons. The future can only see such capabilities increase, and although it may be possible to argue that manned flight over the battle area is becoming so dangerous that remotely piloted vehicles will have to be used, their roles and impact will remain unchanged.

LEFT: *A Panavia Tornado displays its air combat armament: four Sky Flash missiles under the fuselage and a Sidewinder under each wing, next to the fuel drop-tanks.*

ABOVE: *A Supermarine Spitfire of No 310 Squadron, RAF, equipped with a 20mm wing-mounted cannon.*

ABOVE RIGHT: *War-weary North American F-86E Sabre jets line the deck of the carrier USS* Cape Esperance.

RIGHT: *A Lockheed SR-71 Blackbird reconnaissance aircraft of the 99th Strategic Reconnaissance Squadron, USAF, photographed in 1986. Stationed at Mildenhall, in the United Kingdom, the SR-71s of the 99th SRS have the range to monitor potential aggressors throughout Europe and the Middle East.*

PART I

From Biplane to Monoplane

Air Power 1911-1939

INTRODUCTION

When World War I began in high-summer 1914, military air power was in its infancy. The first manned flight in a heavier-than-air machine had been made only 11 years before, and although the achievement of the Wright brothers on that day in December 1903 had been recognized as a technological milestone, the impact upon established armies and navies had been muted. Yet the potential was enormous: for the first time in history, war could be fought from above, adding a third dimension to the use of force.

The most obvious advantage of this new capability lay in observation, for knowledge of an enemy's strength, organization and movement was essential if a commander was to make his countermoves with success. Traditionally, intelligence of this nature had come from scouting units sent ahead of the main force, under orders to observe and report, and by 1914 most major armies had recognized the advantage of using aircraft in this role. Some reservations were expressed – notably that no one flying at 48km/h (30mph) could possibly see with accuracy what was on the ground – but when British and French aircraft contributed significantly to Allied knowledge of German movements through Belgium and northeastern France in August 1914, few could doubt that a new potential had emerged.

Early observation aircraft such as the Avro 504 and BE-2 had their limitations, however, and these became painfully apparent very early on. Some of the problems were purely practical – in a period before the deployment of aircraft-mounted cameras and air-to-ground radios, any information had to be gathered by human sight alone and reported personally to commanders on the ground – but of far more importance was the vulnerability of the machines to defensive fire. No enemy force was likely to ignore attempts being made to observe its dispositions, and although ground fire rarely succeeded in destroying aircraft in flight, it did force pilots to fly higher and (if possible) faster, so rendering their reports less detailed. Many pilots and observers began to arm themselves, initially through a desire to return hostile fire, but then to attack enemy observation machines in the air. Again, results were usually poor, although when the process was taken one stage farther and machine-guns were fitted to the aircraft, enemy machines could be frightened off or even shot down.

At first, such armament was of only limited value – unless the aircraft was a 'pusher,' with its propeller at the back, forward-firing guns had to be positioned above the propeller arc, with all the attendant problems of accuracy and reloading in flight – but when the Dutchman, Anthony Fokker (working for the Germans) perfected his 'interrupter gear,' enabling guns to be fired through the propeller arc without shredding the blades, a new air role quickly emerged. Instead of observation aircraft defending themselves, machine-gun-armed interceptors (or fighters) such as the Fokker E-III could be flown specifically to search out and destroy the enemy's 'eyes' in the sky. Based on ideas that evolved in 1915, as 'fighting scouts' such as the Airco DH-2 tried to protect observation machines, the fighter soon made its mark on the air battles of Europe. Entire squadrons of Sopwith Pups, Nieuport 17s and Albatros D-IIIs took to the air, engaging in aerial 'dogfights' as they vied for 'air supremacy' – defined in 1916 as the ability to use observation aircraft as and when required, free from interception. In the process, major developments in aircraft design took place, with the emphasis on speed, armament and maneuverability, and the great air 'aces' such as the Red Baron (Manfred von Richthofen), Albert Ball and Eddie Rickenbacker caught the public imagination. It was an image of air fighting that was to persist, disguising the often horrific nature of air-to-air combat.

But this was not the only area of development during World War I. Even before that conflict began, Italian airmen, fighting the Turks in North Africa in 1911, had dropped small bombs onto enemy forces, with dramatic results. Such a pattern of attack was repeated by all sides in the early months of the world war, with special attention being paid to troop concentrations, artillery batteries and supply dumps – targets which were presented in a particularly tempting way once the battlefronts had degenerated into stalemate and armies became static. By 1916, most observation aircraft had been fitted with light bombs and ordered to mount 'opportunity attacks' whenever possible, but they suffered from the development of the fighter and proved vulnerable to ground fire as they flew 'low and slow' over enemy positions. It was not until 1918,

LEFT: *An observation balloon of the British Royal Engineers, photographed in 1900. Balloons of this type were used in South Africa during the Boer War.*

ABOVE: *A Blériot Type XI monoplane, based on the aircraft flown across the English Channel by Louis Blériot on 25 July 1909. The Type XI was used by a number of air services in Europe prior to World War I for pilot training; some were taken overseas by Britain's Royal Flying Corps in August 1914 and it was a Blériot XI-2 of No 3 Squadron that flew the RFC's first reconnaissance mission of the war, on 19 August.*

LEFT: *Squadron-Commander Richard Bell-Davies of the Royal Naval Air Service winning a Victoria Cross in 1915 by landing his Nieuport to rescue a crashed colleague behind enemy lines.*

when aircraft designers in both Britain and Germany began to concentrate on specific 'trench fighters,' that purposebuilt ground support machines appeared. Maneuverable, sturdy and well protected by armor plate, aircraft such as the Armstrong Whitworth FK-8 and Junkers CLII represented an official realization that ground attack was a major air role.

If enemy front-line targets could be attacked in this way, it was only logical to search out and destroy similar targets over a wider area. The results might not be as immediate in terms of battlefield advantage, but more distant locations were initially less likely to be defended and, if rear-area railheads, supply routes and transport 'choke-points' could be hit, the enemy would be weakened. As early as 1914, the Russians were experimenting with long-range aircraft capable of delivering 68kg (150lb) bombs, and as the war progressed, all air forces developed a similar capability. In itself, this was a significant air role – for the first time, all aspects of an army in the field were under threat of attack – but its true significance emerged only gradually and had not been fully tested by 1918. In that year, the British armored-warfare specialist Colonel (later Major-General) JFC Fuller put forward his 'Plan 1919,' in

which he envisaged a precise role for ground-attack aircraft, hitting enemy headquarters and communications in support of tank assaults on a selected stretch of front-line. The intention was to create confusion, leading to demoralization and panic among rear-area troops, cutting off the front-line units and weakening their ability to withstand attack. Although it was never tried out, the idea was taken up by German theorists once the war was over: by 1939 it had evolved into the stunningly effective doctrine of *blitzkrieg* ('lightning war'), with the Junkers Ju-87 Stuka dive-bomber in the air role.

A similar pattern of World War I experimentation and postwar theory emerged as the concept of aerial bombardment was extended even farther behind the battleline, deep into the enemy homeland. The idea of dropping bombs onto civilian centers, creating panic and destroying war industries, had entered the public consciousness well before World War I – H G Wells' prophetic novel *The War in the Air* had appeared as early in 1907 – but initial attempts to translate this into reality proved unsuccessful: by the end of 1916, a German campaign against England using Zeppelin airships had been called off because of heavy losses. But in 1917 the Germans decided to use aircraft instead, introducing a speed,

11

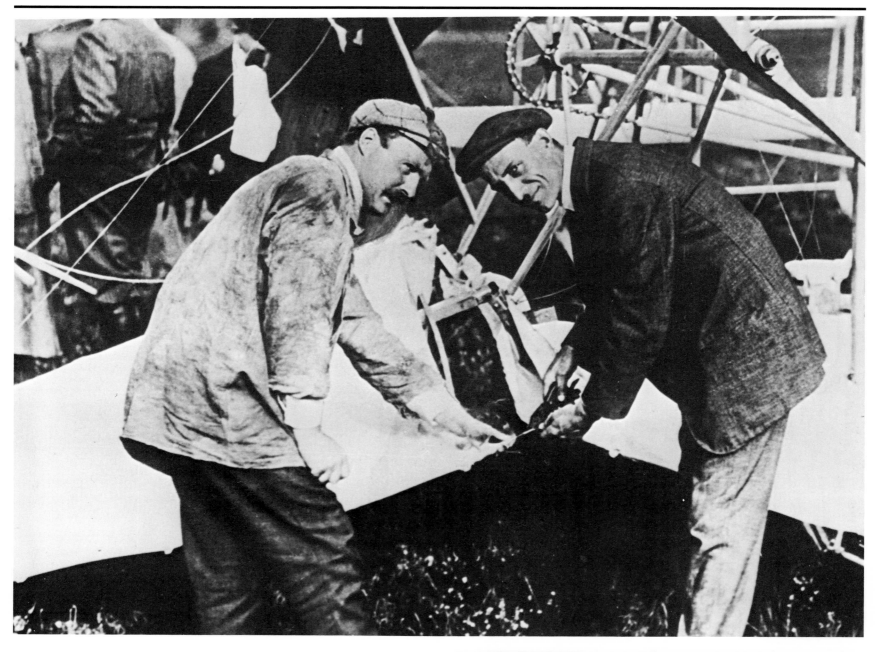

flexibility and hitting power which began significantly to affect British civilian morale. As London fell victim to attacks by Gotha GIV and Zeppelin-Staaken R ('Giant') bombers, signs of panic appeared, war production declined and the government was forced to act. An elaborate ring of antiaircraft guns and fighters was set up around London and, more significantly, a decision was made to mount a counteroffensive against German cities. On 1 April 1918, the Royal Air Force (RAF) was created as an independent body, charged specifically with such attacks.

In the event, the war ended before the theory of strategic bombing had been fully tested, but the seeds of a far-reaching air role had been sown. Although the air-defense system around London enjoyed some success, this was largely ignored by civilians convinced that, in the course of any future war, waves of virtually invulnerable enemy bombers would tear the heart out of major cities, using bombs and gas, in a matter of hours. Fueled by the writings of theorists such as Giulio Douhet and 'Billy' Mitchell, the public ignored the enormous strides in defense – the machine-gun-armed monoplane fighter and the invention of early-warning radar – and insisted on believing the worst. By 1939 strategic bombing was the role that the public associated with air warfare.

But other air roles had been perfected, most notably at sea. Although initially restricted by a dependence on land bases, aircraft began to affect naval warfare during World War I, and by 1918 a number of specifically naval roles had emerged. As in land operations, the first of these was observation, with aircraft flying 'over the horizon' to report the movements of the enemy fleet, but until they could accompany ships to sea, this was somewhat restricted in scope. At first, the emphasis was upon floatplanes, capable of taking off from the sea, but this was too dependent upon calm waters and elaborate launch and recovery procedures to provide an answer. The real breakthrough came in 1917, when the British first experimented with the concept of an aircraft carrier. Created by the simple expedient of welding a flat deck onto an existing hull, the existence of a floating, self-contained airfield with the fleet was potentially revolutionary, enabling naval commanders not simply to observe but also to attack the enemy at long range, using aircraft fitted with bombs and even torpedoes. Once again, the concept had to be further developed, but by 1939 Britain, the United States and Japan had all built and deployed a carrier force. As World War II showed, particularly in the Pacific, the carrier significantly altered the nature and organization of traditional fleets.

This fitted the general trend of air power development, for by 1939 most of the roles of the aircraft in war had been laid down: observation, fighter defense, ground attack, naval support, tactical and strategic bombing. Others had been recognized – for example, the RAF had used transport aircraft to ferry troops and supplies to colonial troublespots in India and the Middle East in the 1920s and 1930s – but were to have their true significance realized only during World War II. Even so, the speed and impact of air power had been remarkable, all taking place within less than 40 years of the first manned flight.

LEFT: *The pioneers of manned flight: the brothers Orville (left) and Wilbur Wright make minor adjustments to their 'Flyer' during a demonstration in 1904.*

BELOW LEFT: *An early experiment in offensive air power: as the pilot of this British aircraft perches precariously on the 'top deck,' his 'gunner' occupies an uncomfortable position below.*

RIGHT: *Colonel Samuel Cody poses beside the shoulder-wing monoplane – the Cody V – which won the British Military Aeroplane Competition in 1912. Allocated the Serial Number 301, the aircraft broke up in the air on 28 April 1913, killing the pilot.*

BELOW: *A Handley Page V/1500 heavy bomber, fitted with four 350hp Rolls-Royce Eagle engines. Built in 1918, the V/1500 never saw active service.*

RECONNAISSANCE

Reconnaissance and Observation
The BE-2

As early as October 1911, engineers such as Frederick Green and Geoffrey de Havilland, working for what would soon become the Royal Aircraft Factory, Farnborough (England), produced the first in a significant series of purposebuilt military aircraft. Taking as their model a Voisin biplane, they designed a successful tractor machine (i.e. one with the propeller at the front) which was named the BE (Blériot Experimental) No. 1. Test-flown by de Havilland on 4 December 1911, it proved to be a reliable and stable aircraft, ideally suited for the primary task of military machines at that time: reconnaissance and observation. It was still flying with the Royal Flying Corps (RFC) as late as July 1916.

But the BE-1 was only an experimental model, and almost immediately it was followed by the BE-2, an aircraft with which elements of the RFC were to go to war in August 1914. The basic design was similar to that of the BE-1, but the fitting of a 60hp Renault engine gave improved performance, including a top speed of 105km/h (65mph) and an impressive service ceiling of 3050m (10,000ft). By late 1912, the British government had placed orders for a number of such aircraft and, over the next two years, these were used to lay down the basic principles of reconnaissance and observation while working in close cooperation with army units on maneuvers in both England and Ireland. At the same time, pilots flying the BE-2 set a number of records, notably that for endurance (7 hours 20 minutes), achieved by Captain C A H Longcroft in November 1913.

Such a potential for lengthy flight was clearly valuable in terms of reconnaissance and observation, giving the pilot plenty of time to build up a comprehensive picture of enemy dispositions, but there was more to it than that. If the pilot was flying alone, without an observer (something that was essential if extra fuel was to be carried), he had to be free to observe and make notes, avoiding any need to concentrate on his machine. The BE design proved particularly well suited to this requirement, especially after modifications in May 1914 had produced the BE-2c. By mounting

ABOVE: *Lieutenant W Leefe Robinson pushes his BE-2c to its limits as he shoots down a Zeppelin airship over England, 3 September 1916. Although not designed for interception, the BE-2 proved to be an adaptable, if rather limited, machine.*

LEFT: *A Vickers Fighting Biplane (FB) 'Gunbus,' showing the advantages of a 'pusher' design – the front mounting for a machine-gun was useful protection as the sky became hostile. Unfortunately, 'pusher' designs lacked the power needed as more conventional 'tractor' machines developed.*

FAR LEFT: *A sergeant of the Royal Flying Corps checks the camera on a BE-2, prior to a reconnaissance mission. The unwieldy nature of the camera may be appreciated.*

staggered mainplanes, fitted with ailerons, as well as a rectangular tail-fin, the 2c virtually flew itself. Indeed, one of the early pilots, Sefton Brancker, reported that when he traveled from Farnborough to the RFC base at Netheravon on 9 June 1914, he did so without even touching the controls between take-off and landing, spending all his time making copious notes about the country over which he flew. Hardly surprisingly, substantial orders (for the time) were placed by the British government for the aircraft, and although only a few 2cs had appeared in France by early 1915, it was apparent that a stable observation platform had emerged. By the end of the year, 119 BE-2cs were serving on the Western Front.

The worth of the BE design had already been proved, however, for it was pilots flying the basic BE-2 who, in August and September 1914, provided Field Marshal Sir John French, Commander-in-Chief of the British Expeditionary Force, with invaluable information about German movements during the early, crucial phase of mobile operations. Thereafter, as new engines and wing designs produced the 2a, 2b, 2c and 2d, the aircraft was used not only for reconnaissance but also for artillery spotting and even rudimentary bombing. Unfortunately, as 'fighting scouts' and purposebuilt fighters emerged, the BE-2 began to suffer significant limitations, caused ironically by its stability in the air. Although various experiments were put into effect, no armament fixture seemed to provide an adequate defense against enemy interceptors: the BE-2 lacked the maneuverability for successful 'dogfighting.' During the 'Fokker Scourge' of 1915-16, the BE design suffered heavy losses, destroying its value in its chosen role.

Nevertheless, the BE-2 proved sufficiently versatile to maintain its front-line deployment. As early as 26 April 1915, Second Lieutenant W B Rhodes Moorhouse won a Victoria Cross (the first for air action) when he gallantly pressed home a bombing attack on Courtrai railway station in a BE-2c, despite having been badly wounded. On 3 September 1916, Lieutenant W Leefe Robinson won a similar award for shooting down a Zeppelin airship at night over England, and although in this case his BE-2c had been pushed to its limits, particularly in terms of altitude, it proved sturdy enough to do the job. By then, however, it was obvious that the drawbacks to the design were critical. Some BE-2s continued to see service throughout the remainder of the war, but they could only operate if heavily protected or in a situation of Allied air supremacy. Stability and endurance were all very well, but survivability against enemy fighters was, by 1916, the key to success in a demanding role.

BE-2c

Type: Two-seater reconnaissance/observation biplane.
Performance: Max speed 120km/h (75mph).
Service ceiling 1982m (6500ft).
Endurance 3 hours 15 minutes.
Armament: From one to four 7.92mm (0.303in) Lewis machine-guns on a variety of (unsatisfactory) mountings.

LEFT: *An FE-2b of No 100 Squadron, RFC, prepares for a night raid. This particular aircraft was destroyed in action on 25 January 1918.*

ABOVE RIGHT: *A BE-2c awaits squadron delivery, early 1916. By then, the design was outmoded, chiefly because it proved difficult to arm.*

BELOW RIGHT: *A Royal Flying Corps officer – on secondment from the Royal Artillery – stands beside his Reconnaissance Experimental (RE) 8, 1916. The RE-8 was the first RFC reconnaissance machine to be designed specifically to defend itself: the ring mounting for the Lewis gun may be clearly seen.*

BELOW: *A Blériot Experimental (BE) 2a reconnaissance machine is prepared for flight, 1913.*

THE FIGHTER

The Evolution of the Fighter
The Fokker E-III

Der neue Fokker-Eindecker
für Rückenflüge

In 1914, the major European powers were equipped with aircraft of widely differing designs, reflecting the experimental nature of flying at that time. Both single-wing monoplanes and double-wing biplanes were in use, and although the former were all 'tractor' designs, with the propeller at the front, the latter were a mix of both 'tractors' and 'pushers' (with the propeller at the back). It did not take long for air commanders to realize that such diversity caused nightmares of supply and maintenance, and by early 1915 attempts were being made to impose uniformity, at least within individual squadrons. Unfortunately, in the absence of centrally controlled design and manufacturing, uniformity proved impossible.

So long as the roles of aircraft comprised nothing more than reconnaissance and observation, this did not really matter in tactical terms, but once the decision had been made to arm those aircraft, either for protection or offensive action, significant problems emerged. The most effective armament was undoubtedly the machine-gun, giving the range and firepower needed for the destruction of an enemy in flight, but not every aircraft provided a suitable firing platform. Pusher biplanes were the easiest to arm – a machine-gun could be fitted to the observer's position in the nose, giving an unimpeded field of fire – and it was possible to provide

LEFT: *A Fokker E-111, shown without its forward-firing guns but displaying its monoplane construction well. This is probably a prototype undergoing tests.*
ABOVE: *Captain Oswald Boelcke, the legendary German fighter 'ace.' He destroyed 40 Allied aircraft in combat.*

19

similar guns on flexible mountings in the 'back seat' of a tractor design, although the latter had limitations of direction and arc: forward-firing was impossible because of the engine and (on a biplane) the top wing, while rearward arcs were impeded by the tailplane. What was needed was some way of achieving forward firing in all designs, preferably with the guns under the control of the pilot, who could aim his aircraft and choose the right moment for action to begin.

This became essential as aircraft designers laid more and more emphasis on tractor machines – the pushers had limitations of maneuverability – for any forward-firing gun would inevitably destroy the propeller blades. In the RFC, attempts were made to get round the problem by fitting guns onto the top wing, above the propeller arc and just within reach of the pilot, but these were very difficult to aim and, until special backward-sliding mountings had been added, almost impossible to reload or unjam without the pilot losing control of his aircraft. At the same time, the French conducted experiments with metal deflector plates, riveted on to the propeller blades: these, as their name implies, were meant to deflect bullets away from the propeller, it being presumed that enough would get through the 'gaps' between the blades to provide an adequate weight of fire. But this had its drawbacks: quite often, the deflector plates were not strong enough or their weight affected the stability of the propeller. Something more trustworthy was clearly needed.

This was provided by Anthony Fokker, a Dutch designer working for the Germans, in 1915 and, like so many brilliant inventions, was remarkably simple. He worked on the principle that the fire of the machine-gun should be stopped every time a propeller blade came in front of the barrel: this would avoid the problem of weighty deflector plates and ensure that nothing would hit the propeller at any time. He therefore added a cam to the back of the propeller

boss, with 'teeth' behind each blade; as the blade came round, the teeth would push down a special arm, automatically disengaging the machine-gun trigger until the blade had passed. As this would happen very quickly and the arm would be released as soon as the blade was out of danger, the rate of fire would not be drastically reduced. It worked well, being disrupted only by unconnected problems such as faulty ammunition or defective guns.

The Germans received the first of the 'interrupter gears' in August 1915, mounted on the front fuselage of Fokker E-III monoplanes. These flimsy-looking aircraft, powered by single 100hp Oberursel U1 piston engines, had a dramatic effect on the balance of power in the air above the Western Front, proving to be both nimble and destructive, especially in the hands of 'aces' such as Oswald Boelcke and Max Immelmann. The Allies had nothing to equal the impact of forward-firing guns, with the result that for almost a year they had to endure the 'Fokker Scourge,' losing aircraft after aircraft and being denied the ability to observe enemy ground movements in key sectors of the front. It was to take the introduction of Nieuport 11 and DH-2 purposebuilt fighters to redress some of the balance in the spring 1916, but no Allied plane could be fitted with its own interrupter gear until an E-III had been captured intact on 8 April. Air warfare had entered a new era.

Fokker E-III
Type: Single-seat fighting scout.
Performance: Max speed 140km/h (87.5mph).
Service ceiling 3500m (11,485ft).
Endurance 90 minutes.
Armament: One (sometimes two) forward-firing synchronized LMG 08 7.92mm (0.303in) machine-guns.

TOP LEFT: *A modern replica of a Fokker E-III in flight. In 1915-16, the impact of the E-III was enormous: its forward-firing machine-guns, using the 'interrupter gear' perfected by Anthony Fokker, rendered all other existing aircraft extremely vulnerable. For the first time, the pilot was able to fly toward his target, line it up in his sights and fire his twin machine-guns with impressive accuracy.*

LEFT: *A German Fokker D-VII, of the type issued to front-line fighter squadrons in 1918. By November 1918, almost 65 percent of German fighters on the Western Front were D-VIIs: despite the existence of excellent Allied 'fighting scouts' by that time, the D-VII was well respected in combat, particularly when flown by men such as Ernst Udet and Hermann Goering.*

RIGHT: *Close-up of the armament of a Fokker Dr-1 triplane: two fixed 7.92mm LMG 08/15 machine-guns, fitted with an interrupter gear for forward firing. An exceptionally nimble fighting scout, the Dr-1 is best remembered as the mount of Manfred von Richthofen – the 'Red Baron' – although he actually preferred an Albatros D-III. Triplane designs were unusual and were subject to a number of accidents.*

Air Fighting in World War I
The Nieuport 17

The concept of the fighter aircraft, designed specifically to achieve or maintain air supremacy by destroying enemy observation machines and their escorts, had begun to emerge by 1916. German squadrons, equipped with Fokker E-III monoplanes and the revolutionary forward-firing machine-guns, had held sway over the trenches of the Western Front since mid-1915, but the Allies were gradually redressing the balance with the deployment of 'fighting scouts.' Among the latter was a series of biplanes, manufactured by the French firm of Nieuport and designed by the naval engineer Gustave Delage.

Interest in Nieuport designs dated back to 1911, when examples of a monoplane, powered by a single 50hp Gnome engine, were tested for military purposes by both the French and British armies. Although distrusted after a series of accidents to other monoplane machines, subsequent Nieuport biplane designs were purchased and deployed, particularly by the British Royal Naval Air Service (RNAS) and RFC. Not all the designs proved entirely satisfactory – according to a test-pilot report on the Nieuport 12 in 1916, the aircraft was so heavy and underpowered that it was 'dangerous to fly' – but Delage persisted, modifying his basic design until the problems were ironed out. When he added a 110hp Le Rhône engine to his normal airframe in 1916, he came up with a 'fighting scout' that was sturdy, mechanically reliable and capable of taking on contemporary German machines.

BELOW: *Nieuport 17s and 24s of No 1 Squadron, RFC, at Bailleul on the Western Front, winter 1917. The nearest aircraft is a Nieuport 24, with its more streamlined tail-fin; the one behind it is a 17. Although the 17 could be fitted with a forward-firing machine-gun on the nose, most were fitted with a single Lewis gun set to fire over the propeller, as shown.*

ABOVE: *A remarkable in-flight photograph of a French aircraft, showing the pilot and his observer high above the flat lands of Flanders. The observer is armed with a drum-fed Lewis gun, and his restricted field of fire may be appreciated: he cannot engage targets immediately to the rear because of the tail-fin and wires, and he cannot fire forward because of the pilot and engine.*

LEFT: *Captain William Bishop, photographed in the cockpit of his Nieuport 17. A Canadian who transferred to the RFC in July 1915, Bishop was a ruthless fighter pilot: his ultimate score of 72 victories placed him second only to Major Edward Mannock (73 victories) in the British list of 'aces.' Bishop was awarded a Victoria Cross for his actions on 2 June 1916, when he carried out a solo dawn attack on an enemy airfield, shooting down three German scouts as they rose to intercept him and destroying others on the ground. He survived the war and remained in the Royal Canadian Air Force for many years: he died in 1956.*

ABOVE: *A Nieuport 28 (replica), shown in the colors of the 94th Aero Squadron ('Hat in the Ring'), American Expeditionary Force, March 1918. Lack of American success with this aircraft was to lead to a switch to the SPAD VII in July 1918.*

LEFT: *A Nieuport 17 of the French Lafayette Escadrille: note the top-wing mounted drum-fed Lewis gun, complete with handle to pull down for reloading the magazine in flight. French air 'aces' such as Georges Guynemer and Charles Nungesser scored highly in 17s.*

TOP RIGHT: *A British SE-5a fighting scout in flight, showing its unusual armament: a single fixed 0.303in Vickers on the fuselage, fitted with interrupter gear, and a 0.303in Lewis on Foster wing-mounting.*

RIGHT: *A rather garish Nieuport 17 of an American squadron, photographed in 1918. The idea of camouflage was not accepted during World War I; it was thought that bright colors would intimidate the enemy.*

In British service, the RFC began to receive examples of this new model – the Nieuport 17 – in mid-July 1916 and, after evaluation, orders were placed for more than 100 to be purchased. Some delays were experienced, caused chiefly by a shortage of engines, but by the end of the year a number of RFC squadrons on the Western Front had been fully equipped. Officially designated a 'sesquiplane' (i.e. an aircraft with a much smaller bottom than top wing), the Nieuport 17 enjoyed good lift and low drag, enabling it to achieve a respectable top speed of 172km/h (107mph) at an operating altitude of 2000m (6560ft). The only real drawback lay in its armament, for even at this relatively late stage forward-firing machine-guns, incorporating the 'interrupter gear' perfected by Anthony Fokker, were not standard fit on British or French machines. Instead, they were equipped with single 7.92mm (0.303in) Vickers or Lewis guns on mountings fixed to the top wing of the aircraft. This meant that although they could be fired forward without shredding propeller blades, they were extremely inconvenient in combat, the pilot having to reach upward to fire and reload. Fortunately, by 1916 an ingenious device, named for its inventor, Sergeant R G Foster of

RIGHT: *The pilots of No 1 Squadron, RFC, pose at Clairmarrais with their SE-5a fighting scouts, July 1918. The squadron had converted from Nieuport 17s in January.*

FAR RIGHT: *A Sopwith Pup fighting scout is prepared for take-off, 1919. The Pup, introduced in 1916, was renowned for its maneuverability in flight.*

BELOW: *A SPAD VII fighting scout in French colors, 1917. British pilots found the SPAD less satisfactory than their French colleagues, preferring the Nieuport.*

No. 11 Squadron, RFC, had been perfected, whereby the gun could be lowered rearward for reloading, and this did make a significant difference, particularly when it had the added advantage of enabling the pilot to fire directly upward in the complex maneuvers of a dogfight Experiments with other armaments fit did take place, but the Nieuport 17 proved unsuited to fuselage-mounted guns.

Nevertheless, it proved a popular machine, chiefly because it gave Allied pilots a slight edge over existing enemy designs, at least until the appearance of purposebuilt fighters such as the Albatros D-III in late 1916. During that brief period of Allied advantage, the Nieuport 17 acted as favorite mount to a number of the early air 'aces' – those pilots whose skill and daring led them to

amass 'scores' of enemy aircraft destroyed. In British service, the first of these to emerge was Albert Ball, who shot down 44 enemy machines between August 1916 and his death in combat 10 months later: he was particularly adept at using the Foster mounting for upward-firing attacks. By the time of his death, other 'aces' had joined him in exploiting the merits of the Nieuport 17 – the Canadian William Bishop, the Frenchman Georges Guynemer and the Belgian André de Meulemeester. Although rendered dangerously obsolete by the German fighters of 1917, the Nieuport 17 continued in front-line service for a number of months, after which it was relegated to training duties, particularly with the American Expeditionary Force in France in 1918. As an interim 'fighting scout,' it occupies an important place in the history of air combat; without it, many of the 'aces' now so familiar to us would probably not have opened their scores.

Nieuport 17
Type: Single-seat fighting scout.
Performance: Max speed 172km/h (107mph).
Service ceiling 2000m (6560ft).
Endurance 2 hours.
Armament: One (sometimes two) fixed 7.92mm (0.303in) Vickers or Lewis machine-guns on Foster mounting.

ABOVE: *Captain Albert Ball, the first British 'ace' to receive national publicity. Something of a loner, he had amassed a score of 44 victories by the time of his death.*
LEFT: *Norman Arnold's watercolor* The Last Fight of Captain Ball, VC, DSO, MC, 17th May, 1917. *Among Ball's opponents in his final engagement was Lothar von Richthofen, brother of the 'Red Baron.'*

The 'Red Baron'
The Albatros D-III

Baron Manfred von Richthofen, known to his enemies as the 'Red Baron' from the color of his favorite aircraft, an Albatros D-III fighting scout, was the most famous of the air 'aces' in World War I. His eventual score of 80 confirmed aerial victories, most of them achieved in 1917-18, was unsurpassed in any of the rival air forces and his contribution to the growing art of air-to-air combat was substantial. He, above all others, came to epitomize the new gladiators of war, free from the horrors of trench deadlock and dedicated to the less restricted role of conflict in the air.

Von Richthofen was born in 1892 and, from an early age, was destined for a military career. Commissioned into the crack cavalry unit, the 1st Uhlan Regiment, in 1912, he transferred to the *Fliegertruppe* (flying service) two years later. Like many other men who were to become aces, his record at first was an undistin-

guished one: in August 1915 he was posted as an observer to serve on board AEG biplane bombers flying over Allied front-line positions in Flanders. Underpowered and capable of only short-range bombing missions, the AEGs were not the most glamorous of mounts and, after less than two months, von Richthofen successfully applied for pilot training, having been inspired by the incomparably skillful fighter ace, Oswald Boelcke. After service as a bomber pilot on both the Western and Eastern Fronts, von Richthofen was chosen by Boelcke to join the newly formed *Jagdstaffel* (*Jasta*) 2: he achieved his first confirmed aerial victory in September 1916, having had the priceless benefit of personal tuition from Boelcke, whose death less than a month later was to rob Germany of one of its best and most natural air-combat flyers.

Jasta 2 was, in fact, the first purpose-designed fighter squadron

BELOW: *An Albatros D-V, showing its streamlined fuselage and partly exposed engine. Armed with two fixed 7.92mm LMG 08/15 machine-guns in the nose, the Albatros was a useful fighter.*

to appear in World War I. Formed in August 1916 under Boelcke's command, it was an attempt to create a unit dedicated to the destruction of Allied observation machines over the trenches of the Western Front and represented a logical extension of the growing realization that air supremacy could be fought for and achieved. Renamed *Jasta Boelcke* after its founder's death in October 1916, it acted not only as a center for innovation but also as a valuable training ground for other air leaders. By January 1917, when he was transferred to command *Jasta 11* at Douai, von Richthofen had already gained a total of 16 confirmed kills and was about to be awarded the coveted *Pour le Mérite* ('Blue Max'), Germany's highest bravery medal at the time.

Albatros D-III
Type: Single-seat fighting scout.
Performance: Max speed 165km/h (103mph).
Service ceiling 5700m (18,700ft).
Endurance 2 hours.
Armament: Two fixed 7.92mm (0.303in) LMG 08/15 machine-guns, fitted with interrupter gear for forward firing.

RIGHT: *Manfred von Richthofen, the greatest 'ace' of World War I, with 80 victories to his credit.*

When von Richthofen took over his new command, it comprised a total of 12 pilots but had no record of aerial success. By April 1917 – a month known to the British as 'Bloody April' after their loss of 730 airmen – *Jasta 11*'s score had rocketed to 88 enemy aircraft. By then, von Richthofen's personal tally had reached 49 and his reputation, enhanced by a decision to paint his aircraft bright red (a ploy designed not only to frighten the enemy but also to ensure easy recognition by fellow *Jasta* pilots in the confusion of battle) had spread far and wide. His own tactical skills, based upon a realization that height always conferred an advantage over an adversary and that a cool nerve invariably ensured survival, were undeniably good, but without access to the Albatros D-III biplane fighting scout, his score would probably have been less. Designed for the specific task of achieving air supremacy, the Albatros proved to be one of the best aircraft of World War I, providing the *Jasta* pilots with a mount worthy of their fast developing talents. Flown by men such as von Richthofen, his brother Lothar and the young Hermann Goering (head of the Luftwaffe in World War II), it became the scourge of Allied air forces for most of 1917, being countered only by the development and deployment of the SE-5 and SPAD fighters later in the year.

Manufactured by the Albatros Werke GmbH, the Albatros D series began life in 1916, when the D-I model first appeared. Its streamlined cigar-shaped fuselage, created by pinning plywood panels to a wooden framework, gave the aircraft enhanced speed and maneuverability, and although problems were encountered during the early stages of development with the wings, which had a disturbing habit of breaking up in a dive, it was seen that the design had potential. By October 1916 the D-I had given way to the D-II, with strengthened wings and enhanced pilot visibility, but it was the D-III, introduced in January 1917, that created a truly effective fighting machine. Based in part on German examination of a captured Nieuport scout, the D-III incorporated lengthened upper wings (and shortened lower ones) to increase maneuverability, as well as special 'V' struts to separate the wings and further strengthen them under the pressure of combat dives. Powered by a 175hp Mercedes D-IIIa six-cylinder in-line engine, the top of which was exposed for cooling and easy access, the new aircraft was capable of a speed of 165km/h (103mph) and, importantly

BELOW: *A Fokker Dr-1 triplane is moved into position for take-off, using both horse and manpower. The primitive conditions of a World War I fighter station are well illustrated.*

ABOVE: *An Albatros D-III, distinctive in its silver livery and black lightning marking, stands on display at a present-day air show. This example is probably a replica.*

RIGHT: *A Hawker Hart light day-bomber of the RAF. Capable of a top speed of 296km/h (184mph), the Hart was faster than most fighters when it entered service in 1930, highlighting the need for improved fighter designs.*

BELOW RIGHT: *A formation of Boeing P-26A 'Peashooter' pursuit aircraft of the US Army Air Corps' 20th Pursuit Group, photographed in 1936. Monoplane construction gave the P-26 both speed and altitude, but the fixed undercarriage was a drawback. It was normally armed with two 0.3in machine-guns.*

BELOW: *A Bristol Bulldog II of No 3 Squadron, RAF, 1929. Powered by a 490hp Bristol Jupiter engine, the Bulldog could achieve a maximum speed of 280km/h (174mph). It was armed with twin Vickers machine-guns and could carry four 9kg (20lb) bombs.*

RIGHT: *Heinkel He-51 biplane fighters of the newly emergent Luftwaffe, 1933. The first fighter openly ordered by the Germans, in defiance of the terms of the Treaty of Versailles, the He-51 was a robust and well produced machine, but it suffered poor speed and rate of climb when pitted against the Polikarpov I-15 in the Spanish Civil War (1936-39). By the beginning of World War II, it had been relegated to training duties.*

BELOW: *A Polikarpov I-16 monoplane fighter, of the type supplied by the Soviets to the Republicans in Spain during the Civil War. Although of unusual appearance, the I-16 had exceptional maneuverability for its time and fought well in both Spain in 1936 and in the Far East in 1939. It was one of the first aircraft to feature a retractable undercarriage.*

LEFT: *Czech Avia B-534 biplane fighters, 1936. At the time, the B-534 Series was considered to be the best ever designed, incorporating a streamlined fuselage and an impressive armament of four 7.7mm machine-guns. But the biplane design still predominated, at a time when most other manufacturers were beginning to realize the advantages of monoplane construction, and the non-retractable undercarriage did produce drag, made worse by the distinctive radiator mounted between the wheel struts. Even so, with a maximum speed of 405km/h (252mph), the B-534 was not an aircraft to be ignored. It was still in use with the Slovak Air Force in 1944.*

bombers could race ahead, out of range. New fighter designs offering better performance were urgently needed.

The answer lay in a combination of new manufacturing techniques and a move away from biplane toward monoplane configuration. By the mid-1930s, spurred on by a desire to produce aircraft capable of winning highly prestigious international air races, designers had begun to realize the advantages to be gained from aerodynamic flow, producing aircraft with light alloy skins instead of fabric. At the same time, in an effort to save weight (needed for more powerful engines and extra fuel), many 'racers' were produced as monoplanes, and once this happened, it was obvious that all the traditional distrust displayed about such designs – based on the high accident rate among monoplanes during World War I – was misplaced. As speed, maneuverability and rate of climb increased dramatically among the racers, the potential in terms of fighter capability could not be ignored.

First in the field were the Germans, responding to the needs of the newly formed Luftwaffe in 1934. Although most of the big manufacturers, including Arado, Focke Wulf and Heinkel, submitted designs, it was the relatively small firm of Bayerische Flugzeugwerke (Bf) AG that came up with a winner. Under the fine leadership of Willi Messerschmitt, a two-seater monoplane – the Bf-108 – had been developed for the 4th *Challenge de Tourisme Internationale* in 1934, and although it did not win, it provided a pattern for a subsequent fighter, the Bf-109. First flown in September 1935, the 109 was a single-seat monoplane, built around the most powerful engine then available – the 680hp Junkers Jumo 210. Initial Luftwaffe reaction was muted – the high undercarriage legs gave the aircraft an angle on the ground which restricted pilot view during take-off – but when production 109Bs achieved a top speed of 465km/h (289mph), displayed impressive rate of climb and excellent maneuverability and played host to four 7.92mm (0.303in) machine-guns (two on the front fuselage and one in each wing), no

---

Hawker Hurricane Mark I

Type: Single-seat monoplane fighter.
Performance: Max speed 509km/h (316mph).
Service ceiling 10,120m (33,200ft).
Max range 740km (460 miles).
Armament: Eight 7.92mm (0.303in) machine-guns.

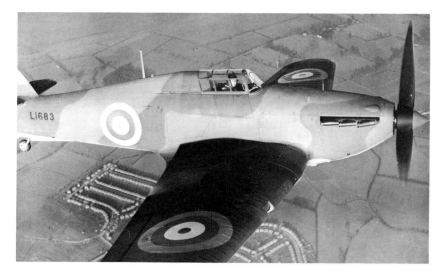

LEFT: *An early example of the Hawker Hurricane monoplane fighter, photographed in 1938. The gap between the airscrew and engine cowling is caused by the thrust tolerance on the propeller shaft.*

RIGHT: *Hawker Hurricane I fighters of No 111 Squadron, RAF Fighter Command, Northolt, 1938. No 111 Squadron was the first to be equipped with the Hurricane: after working up on the new machines, it was ready for service by the time of the Munich Crisis in late 1938.*

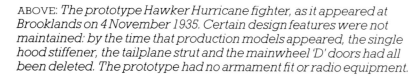

ABOVE: *The prototype Hawker Hurricane fighter, as it appeared at Brooklands on 4 November 1935. Certain design features were not maintained: by the time that production models appeared, the single hood stiffener, the tailplane strut and the mainwheel 'D' doors had all been deleted. The prototype had no armament fit or radio equipment.*

ABOVE: *Messerschmitt Bf-109B-1 of the Condor Legion, early 1937. The problems experienced by the Heinkel He-51 fighters in Spain, particularly when they encountered Republican Polikarpov I-15s, forced the Germans to re-equip their Condor Legion squadrons, supporting the Nationalists. The Bf-109B, with its speed, agility and 7.92mm armament, soon redressed the balance.*

RIGHT: *A Bf-109B of the Condor Legion flies low over a Republican position in Spain, 1938. Although deployed principally in the fighter role, the 109 was equally adept at low-level ground attack.*

FAR RIGHT, TOP: *Dr Willi Messerschmitt, one of Germany's most inventive and prolific aircraft designers. Born in 1898, he began designing gliders and sailplanes in 1912, when he was only 14 years old. In 1927 he became chief designer at the Bayerische Flugzeugwerke in Augsburg, where he was responsible, among other projects, for the single-engine Bf-109 and twin-engine Bf-110 fighters.*

FAR RIGHT, BOTTOM: *A Bf-109B-1 photographed in the early summer of 1937, probably while undergoing acceptance trials for the Luftwaffe. The clean lines of the design may be clearly seen.*

one could deny that a formidable new machine had emerged. The Messerschmitt Bf-109 was to remain in production, suitably modified in ways which would reflect the advances of new technology, throughout World War II.

The British did not lag far behind, producing their first monoplane fighter – the Hawker Hurricane – in November 1935. This, in fact, had its origins as early as 1933, when a monoplane version of the highly acclaimed Hawker Fury was suggested, but delays in the manufacture of new Rolls-Royce Merlin engines occurred. As soon as the prototype took to the air, however, it became apparent that the Hurricane was going to be something special: with a top speed of 509km/h (316mph) it outclassed even the Bf-109. The Mark I entered RAF service in late 1937, offering all the attributes of an effective fighter – speed, impressive rate of climb and an armament fit of eight 7.92mm (0.303in) machine-guns (four in each wing). By 1939, a total of 497 Hurricanes had been delivered to Fighter Command, and although subsequent attempts to improve the design were disappointing (by 1942 the Hurricane had been shifted to night-fighter and fighter-bomber roles), the Mark I acted as the mainstay of British air-defense throughout the Battles of France and Britain in 1940. When used in conjunction with the Supermarine Spitfire (first flown in March 1936), it was formidable.

Messerschmitt Bf-109B

Type: Single-seat monoplane fighter.
Performance: Max speed 465km/h (289mph).
Service ceiling 8200m (26,900ft).
Max range 692km (430 miles).
Armament: Four 7.92mm (0.303in) machine-guns.

BOMBING

The Origins of Strategic Bombing
The Gotha G-IV

In October 1914, only two months after the outbreak of World War I, Major Wilhelm Siegert of the Imperial German Army received permission to train a squadron of single-engine Taube bombers for operations against the ports of southern England. Airfields around Calais were earmarked for use as bases in what would have been the first deliberate bombing of an enemy homeland: fortunately for the British, Calais remained in Allied hands and the project had to be canceled.

But a seed had been sown and, lacking aircraft of sufficient range, the Germans turned instead to the Zeppelin airships belonging primarily to the navy. They carried out their first raid on the night of 19/20 January 1915, when two of their number dropped bombs on King's Lynn in Norfolk, and this heralded a campaign which was to continue, in spasmodic fashion, for nearly two years. It never developed into a sustained offensive – the Zeppelins, floating across the North Sea from bases in northern Germany, were slow, their navigation was poor and, once the British had organized a response, they proved vulnerable to fighter attack – and by late 1916, rather than face the deteriorating winter weather, the raids were quietly phased out. Very little material damage had been inflicted, but significant signs of civilian panic had been discerned by the British authorities.

LEFT: *Searchlights on Old Lambeth Bridge, London, 1914: the lack of a blackout is noticeable.*
RIGHT: *American troops, equipped with a French Hotchkiss machine-gun, keep watch for enemy planes, Raucort, France, 1918.*
BELOW: *Zeppelin L12: this airship passed over Margate, Deal and Ramsgate on 9 August 1915, but inflicted little damage.*

The Germans did not abandon the idea of aerial bombardment, they merely altered the means of carrying it out. As early as 1915, various manufacturers had been instructed to produce purpose-built long-range bombers, capable of carrying up to 500kg (1102lb) of bombs on a round trip of 500km (311 miles). A number of designs for a *Grosskampfflugzeug* ('battleplane') had been submitted, of which the most promising was that produced by Gotha – a twin-engine biplane of conventional design, fully able to satisfy the desired requirements. Small numbers of Gotha G-II and G-III

ABOVE: *As a Gotha G-IV is prepared for its next mission over England, mechanics pose with a range of bombs. Each Gotha could carry between 300 and 500kg (661 and 1102lb) of bombs, depending on the range of the mission. The bombs on show are (from left to right): 20kg (44lb), 50kg (110lb), 100kg (220lb), another 20kg (44lb) and 200kg (440lb).*

FAR RIGHT: *Crew members look out from the forward section of a Gotha G-V. The man in the nose is occupying the forward gun position, which would normally hold a single 7.92mm machine-gun on a pivotal mount. Behind him sits the pilot, who would not be accompanied, and behind him would be a second gunner, also with a single 7.92mm machine-gun. The extra wheels at the front of the main undercarriage are there to prevent the aircraft nosing into the ground on landing: a necessary precaution.*

RIGHT: *A Gotha G-IV receives its bomb-load: in this case, five 50kg (110lb) bombs, in the process of being fitted beneath the wings, and two 100kg (220lb) bombs, already in place under the fuselage. The 'lozenge' camouflage pattern of the Gothas may be seen.*

models appeared in 1915, acting as test-beds for further development and, after trials on the Eastern Front, various improvements were made. The result was the Gotha G-IV – the first successful long-range bomber to be produced – and examples began to arrive in front-line squadrons toward the end of 1916. Powered by two 260hp Mercedes DIVa six-cylinder piston engines, the G-IV could carry the stipulated 500kg (1102lb) of bombs, flying at an operating height of 4500m (15,000ft). Protected by two 7.92mm (0.303in) machine-guns in nose and dorsal positions, and capable of a respectable speed of 140km/h (87mph), it seemed to offer all the advantages which the Zeppelins had lacked. By early 1917, 30 of the Gothas had been delivered to an airfield near Ghistelles in occupied Belgium, where Captain Ernst Brandenburger was forming a special 'England Squadron.'

The bombers were ready for operations by May 1917 and, on the 25th, 21 machines took off for a raid on London. They did not arrive – a combination of mechanical problems, cloudy weather and poor navigation forced them to divert to secondary targets – but the sudden appearance of aircraft in daylight caught British defenses off guard. Nearly five tons of bombs were dropped on Folkestone, killing 95 people and injuring 260; although more than 40 fighters took to the air, not one Gotha was engaged. When a similar raid hit Sheerness on 5 June, it was obvious that the new campaign posed a threat which could not be ignored.

This was reinforced only eight days later, when 14 Gothas finally reached London. In clear skies, the bombers flew unmolested over the capital, dropping their loads in apparently random fashion and inflicting significant damage: 162 people were killed (including a number of children caught in a school in Poplar) and 432 injured, leading to near panic in the streets and demands for government action. The fact that no British fighter managed to engage, let alone destroy, the attackers led, quite naturally, to a feeling that nothing could be done to prevent a repetition of such raids, and when, on 7 July, a further 22 Gothas hit London again, killing 57 and injuring 193, fear gripped the public imagination.

ABOVE: *Jan Christian Smuts, the South African soldier and politician who was asked by the British government to report on the aftermath of the Gotha raids on London in 1917. His findings were crucial to the development of theories of strategic bombing.*

RIGHT: *A rare air-to-air shot of a Gotha bomber, just after having dropped its load onto what appears to be a coastal target, probably in France. The advantages of daylight bombing may be appreciated – the target is easy to see – but the vulnerability of the aircraft to ground fire is obvious.*

FAR RIGHT, TOP: *A Zeppelin-Staaken R-VI heavy bomber, of the type used against England in 1918. Known as 'Giant' bombers, for obvious reasons, the R Series machines could each carry 2000kg (4409lb) of bombs.*

FAR RIGHT, BOTTOM: *The way it all started: a British airman leans over the side of his machine to drop an appropriately inscribed bomb onto enemy positions. Accuracy left much to be desired, although this did not lessen the impact of sudden attack.*

BELOW: *An Italian Caproni Ca-41 heavy bomber, photographed in 1918. This triplane design was unusual in a number of ways, not least its sheer size and extremely lofty crew compartment. Powered by 250hp Fiat A piston engines, the Ca-41 could carry a bomb-load of 900kg (1984lb) over a range of 600km (373 miles).*

A special committee was set up under the South African, Jan Christian Smuts, to investigate the problem and to recommend ways of preventing further attacks. Two reports were submitted in August 1917, the first of which led to the creation of the London Air Defence Area (LADA) – a ring of antiaircraft guns and fighter stations protecting the capital. By early 1918, this had proved to be remarkably successful, but it was overshadowed by the second report, which recommended that a counteroffensive should be mounted against German cities, partly in retaliation but also as a means of deterring future attacks on England. This was to lead eventually, in April 1918, to the creation of a single, independent Royal Air Force (RAF), given just such a strategic role.

By then, the German raids had ceased to pose a significant threat. Mechanical problems with the Gothas, the engines of which proved incapable of withstanding the rigors of war, and the growing effectiveness of the LADA defenses led to losses which the Germans could not absorb. This was apparent as early as autumn 1917, when an attempt to create a sustained offensive at night – a series of attacks, put into effect between 24 September and 2 October, known as the 'Raids of the Harvest Moon' – failed to inflict significant damage, even when the Gothas were joined by small numbers of four-engine Zeppelin-Staaken R (*Riesen*) heavy bombers. The end came on 19 May 1918, when 28 Gothas tried to fight their way through the LADA defenses to hit London, only to lose six of their number to gunfire and fighter attack: a prohibitive loss-rate which led to a halting of the campaign. In material terms, the damage to England had been slight and defensive measures had enjoyed some success, but that was not the memory that remained. Instead, people remembered the raids of June and July 1917 as the symbols of a nightmare suddenly coming true – the prospect of indiscriminate aerial bombardment of civilian centers, leading to death, injury and panic. It was an image of future war that was to have a profound effect during the interwar period.

> ### Gotha G-IV
> **Type:** Twin-engine long-range bomber.
> **Performance:** Max speed 140km/h (87mph).
> Service ceiling 4500m (15,000ft).
> Range 500km (311 miles).
> **Bomb-load:** Up to 500kg (1102lb).

Air Defense of England
The Sopwith F-1 Camel

The London Air Defence Area (LADA), initiated in August 1917, was based upon principles already established as part of the earlier response to Zeppelin attacks: a 'mix' of antiaircraft guns (literally artillery pieces deployed to fire fragmentation shells vertically, in the general direction of the enemy), searchlights and interceptor fighters. Some success had been achieved against the airships – on 28 November 1916, for example, two Zeppelins had been destroyed over the east coast of England – but this was more by good luck than good management. LADA was designed from the outset to create a more coordinated response.

As a preliminary move, Brigadier-General E B Ashmore, an artillery officer with flying experience, was appointed to LADA command. He began by concentrating existing antiaircraft batteries to create barriers to the north, south and east of London, backing them up with fighter squadrons and ground-based observers, the latter under orders to provide reports of visual sightings. Sector commanders were appointed to coordinate the system at a local level and an attempt was made to impose priorities of defense, with certain areas kept free from antiaircraft fire to allow fighters to concentrate on aerial interception. The system was initially undermined by the sudden shift of German emphasis to night-time operations, beginning in early September 1917, but the basic organization proved to be sound. As the Gothas built up the momentum of their assaults in the ensuing months, refinements to

RIGHT: *The effects of aerial bombardment: as the smoke clears from a rail marshaling yard, the full scale of the damage can be seen. Although this is, in fact, a tactical rather than a strategic target, it is indicative of the impact of bombing on the economic infrastructure of a country.*

BELOW: *Sopwith F-1 Camel single-seat fighters of the American 148th Aero Squadron line up and their pilots climb aboard, August 1918. The Camel – arguably one of the best fighters produced during World War I – was used as part of the air defense of England in 1917-18, and was even adapted to night-flying. Normally armed with two fixed 0.303in Vickers machine-guns on the nose, with Sopwith-Kauper 'interrupter gear' attached, the Camel could pack a telling punch.*

ABOVE: *Balloons hold aloft special steel cables as part of Britain's air-defense system in 1918. Attacking aircraft, flying at night, would not be able to see the cables and would crash into them; even if the cables were seen, they would force the enemy to fly higher, so disrupting aim.*

LADA were made, producing an air-defense organization which was, for the time, remarkably effective.

Ashmore's main concern was to track and destroy the enemy bombers before they reached London. Ground observers, stationed under likely approach routes to the capital, were trained to distinguish between British and German aircraft types and, after December 1917, responsibility for this rudimentary early-warning task was transferred from the army to the civil police, using ordinary telephone links to report their sightings. By the end of the war in November 1918, this had been developed into an elaborate communications network, with priority lines from observers to sector commanders and from them to a central headquarters in London. There, the reports were collated to create a clear overall picture of the developing raid, enabling orders to be transmitted to anti-aircraft sites and fighter stations: indeed, by late 1918 powerful radio transmitters even allowed direct communication with aircraft in flight. If this proved difficult, fighters could be guided toward the bomber formation by means of flashing searchlights (at night) or giant rotatable arrows on the ground (during the day).

Meanwhile, the mix of guns, searchlights and fighters had been steadily improved, chiefly by ensuring that the priorities of

defense were strictly imposed. By early 1918, any German bombers had to approach London through a belt of coastal antiaircraft guns before entering a zone in which the fighters had precedence. This took them as far as a 'Green Line' on the outskirts of the capital, beyond which the guns took over again, firing 'box barrages' designed to create a wall of fire at predicted altitudes. As the bombers often had no choice but to fly at those altitudes – if they came lower they encountered barrage balloons and steel cables – the results could be devastating. If they survived, the bombers then had to return through the same zones of defense.

Sopwith F-1 Camel

Type: Single-seat fighting scout.
Performance: Max speed 187km/h (116mph).
Service ceiling 6095m (20,000ft).
Endurance 2 hours 30 minutes.
Armament: Two 7.92mm (0.303in) Vickers machine-guns, fixed on the nose, fitted with interrupter gear for forward-firing.

LEFT: *A Sopwith F-1 Camel fighter 'loops the loop' at fairly low altitude. Although a robust machine, the Camel was renowned for its lack of natural flying grace.*

RIGHT: *Major W G Barker, squadron commander of 28 Squadron RFC, poses beside his Sopwith Camel. Barker was a Canadian who flew with the RFC as an observer in 1915. His first success was in France in 1917 but most of his victories were achieved in Italy in 1918.*

BELOW: *The Sopwith Salamander was a development of the Sopwith Snipe, modified for ground-attack duties. Although used in trials, it did not see squadron service.*

LEFT: By 1938-39, the fear of strategic bombing had reached its height, particularly in Britain, still the only country to have experienced the full impact of a sustained bombing campaign. When war with Germany seemed inevitable, the general public, reacting to official pronouncements which included the famous line 'the bomber will always get through,' uttered by Prime Minister Stanley Baldwin in 1932, were convinced that widespread death and destruction were only hours away. Among the many precautionary measures introduced to lessen the impact of the attacks was an official order that all schoolchildren and young mothers should be evacuated from the major cities into the countryside, where there was at least a chance that they would survive. A partial evacuation was carried out during the Munich Crisis in late 1938, but it was a year later, when war was inevitable, that the policy was implemented in earnest. The children shown here, suitably tagged, are waiting for transport to take them to special trains.

The effectiveness of this system was first shown on 28 January 1918, when 13 Gothas flew toward London in clear night skies: although the antiaircraft guns claimed no victims, the ferocity of their barrage (a total of 15,000 shells) dispersed the bombers, forcing all but three to turn back. Equally significantly, one of the Gothas was stalked and destroyed by two Sopwith Camel fighters – the first successful night interception using the LADA organization. The Camel – a squat, sturdy fighter with a reputation for being difficult to fly – had been designed in late 1916 and test-flown in February 1917, but experiments in night-flying had only taken place eight months later. With no previous experience of the nightmare of taking off and landing in the dark, the pilots of No. 44 Squadron, RFC, persevered until, by January 1918, they were remarkably adept. Once they had secured their first victory, the Gotha threat had been effectively blunted. particularly when the Camels developed a further new role – that of 'intruder' operations, following the bombers back to their bases and bombing ground installations. The success of LADA may have been ignored once the war was over and the hysteria of the interwar theories of strategic bombing gained hold, but all the basic principles of air-defense had been worked out: by 1940, against another bomber threat, a similar pattern of response would achieve more lasting glory. As the Second Battle of Britain took place in the summer of that year, the lessons of 1915-18 were put to good use.

LEFT: The aftermath of a Zeppelin raid on Shoreditch, July 1915.

RIGHT: An obvious counter to the threat of air attack was to deploy antiaircraft guns, capable of producing a barrage of fire which would either destroy the enemy machines in flight or, at least, force the pilots to avoid traveling over their intended target area. By 1917, as this photograph shows, most of the major powers had begun to manufacture purposebuilt antiaircraft guns, often mounted on trucks for extra mobility. This German gun-crew is on the lookout for any marauding Allied aircraft close to the front-line in France.

Strategic Bombing Theory
Douhet and Mitchell

When the Smuts Committee submitted its second report to the British government on 17 August 1917, it contained a prediction that was to strike fear into the hearts of its readers. Taking the evidence of the Gotha raids on London in June and July as a base, Smuts argued that: 'The day may not be far off when aerial operations, with their devastation of enemy lands and destruction of industrial and populace centres on a vast scale, may become the principal operations of war, to which the older forms of military and naval operations may become secondary and subordinate. . .' The implications seemed clear: as the Gothas had shown, aircraft had the ability to fly unmolested over enemy cities, threatening civilian and industrial targets which, if destroyed, would tear the heart out of the state, leaving the 'muscles' of the armed forces to wither away at the front line. War had suddenly become a very nasty business indeed.

This theme was taken up by a number of air power theorists in the years immediately after World War I, the most significant of whom were the Italian Giulio Douhet (1869-1930) and the American Brigadier-General 'Billy' Mitchell (1879-1936). Both believed that

the advent of the bomber gave the attacker a new advantage which could not be easily countered, and although they differed in the detail of their views, both contributed to the creation of a popular fear of air attack which, by 1939, had grown almost to the point of hysteria in potentially threatened states.

Douhet was an experienced airman whose principal work, *The Command of the Air*, first appeared in 1927. He based his ideas on a firm belief that aircraft held the key to victory in future war, but he was aware that they could only do so if they enjoyed unfettered 'command of the air,' picking out and destroying precise targets without having to worry about enemy fighters or antiaircraft defenses. His first priority, therefore, was to use massive air fleets over the enemy homeland, partly to lure defending fighters into a battle they could not hope to win (the bombers being fast, maneuverable and heavily armed), but also to concentrate on the destruction of airfields, aircraft factories and gun emplacements which would leave the bombers with complete air supremacy. Once this had been achieved, cities and industrial complexes would be wide open to attack and, faced with the prospect of civilian panic

and economic collapse, the enemy government would be forced to sue for peace. The war would be short, sharp and effective, avoiding the attritional deadlock of World War I.

Mitchell, whose important work *Winged Defense* appeared in 1925, started from a slightly different premise, reflecting the particular strategic needs of the United States. Because the country was situated between two immense oceans, it was unlikely to be directly threatened, but in order to protect its coasts and to ensure a quick response to attacks upon its allies abroad, Mitchell advocated air power as a cheap and immediate defensive measure. In July 1921 he demonstrated his belief in the use of bombers against naval vessels by successfully sinking the ex-German battleship *Ostfriesland* off the coast of Virginia, and although this particular experiment was somewhat discredited by an obvious lack of opposition from the ship itself, it did confirm the potential of aircraft in future war. It also spurred Mitchell on to further his ideas about bombers as long-range instruments of American power, capable of striking targets in enemy homelands which would be far quicker and more effective than military or naval task forces. Nor was

RIGHT: *Brigadier-General Mitchell at the time of his court-martial in 1925. His accusation that the Army and Navy Departments were guilty of 'incompetence, criminal negligence and almost treasonable administration' went too far.*

BELOW: *Colonel William ('Billy') Mitchell occupies the pilot's position in a SPAD two-seater, with a French officer as his observer/gunner, France, 1918. Mitchell had arrived in France in 1917 as part of Major-General John J Pershing's staff, and had been appointed Aviation Officer of the American Expeditionary Force.*

range the only consideration: if the bombers were to operate in areas were opposition could be expected, they had to be self-defending, literally bristling with guns to take on and destroy attacking fighters. Finally, once over the enemy state, they had to be able to find and destroy precise targets, necessitating daylight operations.

The true impact of Douhet and Mitchell is difficult to gauge – both men were court-martialled in their own countries when they tried to impose their views on a sceptical government – but the basic principles behind their theories acted as a key factor in the creation of fear between the two world wars. Nowhere was this more true than in Britain, where the experience of the German raids of 1917-18 and the continued existence of an independent air force dedicated to strategic bombing reinforced a general belief that, in the event of a future war against an air-minded enemy,

FAR LEFT: *General Giulio Douhet, the Italian air-power expert, whose book* The Command of the Air *(1927) was influential in the evolution of strategic-bombing theory.*

LEFT: *The German battleship hulk* Ostfriesland *suffers a near miss during the bombing trials of July 1921. Although the ship was sunk by Mitchell's Martin bombers, no defensive fire was put up and the outcome failed to convince the skeptics.*

RIGHT: *Billy Mitchell faces his court martial.*

BELOW LEFT: *A Handley Page V/1500 heavy bomber in flight over the United States, 1919. Produced too late to see service in World War I, the V/1500 went on to set a number of records.*

RIGHT: *Billy Mitchell (center) looking optimistic at his court-martial, October 1925.*

BELOW: *A phosphorous bomb explodes over a naval target during US Army Air Corps trials, 1923.*

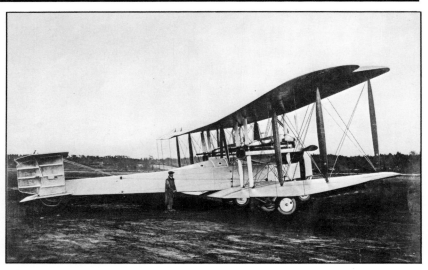

fleets of bombers would appear as if by magic to fly over unprotected cities, raining bombs and poison gas onto the civilian population. As early as 1925, the military theorist Basil Liddell Hart, in his book *Paris or the Future of War*, predicted that, if a war should break out against France, the French Air Force would be able to drop 'a greater weight of bombs . . . on London in one day than in the whole of the Great War,' while seven years later the British prime minister, Stanley Baldwin, publicly confirmed his government's belief that 'the bomber will always get through.' Official statistics of likely losses reflected such fears. By 1938, when the threat was from Nazi Germany with its combat-proven air force, it was declared that over 700,000 casualties a week would result from aerial bombardment, to say nothing of the psychiatric cases caused by people literally going mad under the strain.

In the event, the reality of strategic bombing was to prove far less decisive than the theorists had suggested. Neither Douhet nor Mitchell foresaw the practical problems involved – the lack of aircraft with sufficiently large bomb-loads to inflict the sort of damage

ABOVE: *Captain John Alcock and Lieutenant Arthur Brown, the first men to make a transatlantic flight, 1919.*
ABOVE RIGHT: *Alcock and Brown's Vimy, photographed in 1919. Together with the DH-10 Amiens and Handley Page V/1500, the Vimy arrived too late to see service in World War I.*

envisaged; the enormous improvements to fighter design and the invention of early-warning radar; the remarkable resilience of ordinary people under aerial attack – although this should not be allowed to mask the strength of the interwar beliefs. By the beginning of World War II, it was generally and genuinely felt that massed bombers, flying across enemy territory by day against ineffective defenses, would tear the heart out of a state in the first few hours of war. It was a fear that was to become all too familiar during the nuclear age which was to follow.

ABOVE: *Alcock and Brown's Vimy takes off on its epic flight across the Atlantic, 1919. The prototype Vimy had first flown in November 1917, but only three examples of the machine had reached front-line RAF squadrons by the end of October 1918. Capable of carrying a bomb-load of 1124kg (2476lb) over a range of 1448km (900 miles), it was a powerful machine.*
BELOW: *Australian troops inspect an RAF Handley Page 0/100 heavy bomber. The size of the machine may be appreciated, although it was to be dwarfed by the V/1500 in late 1918.*

The Technology of Air Defense
Radar

The success of the LADA defenses during the last year or so of World War I was initially overlaid by the growing fears about the threat of strategic bombing, but as the peacetime period progressed the possibility of creating an effective and comprehensive air-defense system was revived, particularly in Britain. Antiaircraft guns and searchlights were redeployed around major cities, barrage balloons were brought out of storage and the techniques of fighter protection were reassessed.

But things had changed since 1918. Bombers were faster and capable of much greater range, altitude and hitting power, leaving defenders with distinct disadvantages. Until the development of monoplane fighter designs in the mid-1930s, existing interceptors were often incapable of catching their intended victims, particularly as the methods of providing early-warning were poor. Previous ideas such as ground observers, linked to a central headquarters by civil telephone, may have enjoyed success against Gothas flying at 4500m (15,000ft) and capable of no more than 140km/h (87mph), but when aircraft such as the Dornier Do-17 appeared (after July 1937), with a top speed of 360km/h (224mph) and a service ceiling of 7000m (22,960ft), the use of human observation and reporting became dangerously inadequate. Experiments were carried out using sound locators – literally microphones

mounted in a parabolic reflector and pointed in the direction of engine noise – but by the time these had produced any worthwhile information, the aircraft had flown away. The only answer seemed to lie in the employment of constant standing patrols of interceptors, flying along likely approach routes, but the cost of fuel alone made this potentially prohibitive. By the late 1930s it began to seem as if Stanley Baldwin's assessment that 'the bomber will always get through' was correct.

What was needed by Britain was some method of tracking incoming aircraft, regardless of altitude, speed or weather, for this

ABOVE: *Sir Robert Watson-Watt, the Scots-born physicist credited with inventing radar. By 1935 he had set up an experimental detection system to cover eastern England.*

RIGHT: *A navigator on board a British bomber adjusts his 'Gee' set, 1943. 'Gee' was a navigational aid which worked by means of signals transmitted from ground stations: when these were received inside the aircraft, the navigator could calculate his position fairly accurately by referring to a special chart.*

BELOW: *Part of the British 'Chain Home' radar system, set up in the late 1930s to provide radar detection of incoming enemy aircraft. Some 51 such stations were built, protecting the eastern and southern approaches to England as a priority: each comprised tall masts with the ability to project a radio beam which the hostile aircraft would have to interrupt. By 1939, the system was remarkably efficient.*

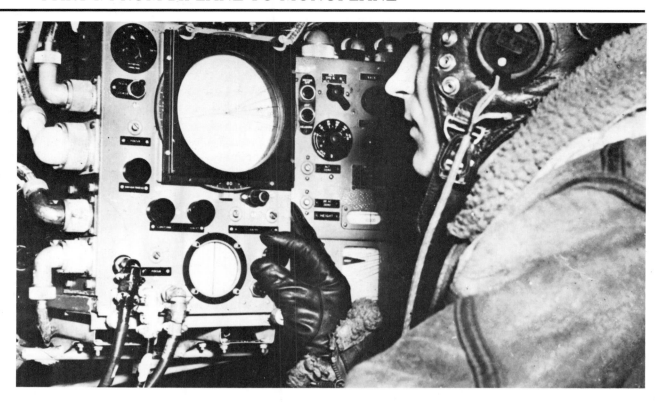

RIGHT: *An Avro Lancaster heavy bomber, photographed in mid-flight, 1944. The bulge beneath the fuselage is the housing for H2S, a navigational aid first developed by British scientists in late 1941. Opposition to its use – it was felt to be too important to risk losing if a carrying aircraft was shot down – delayed its deployment on operations until January 1943, when six H2S-equipped bombers successfully marked targets in Hamburg. H2S worked by reflecting a radar map of the ground into the aircraft: because of its rather crude nature, it was best used over coastal targets, where the difference between land and sea showed up clearly.*

BELOW: *RAF personnel at work plotting ship and aircraft movements. Judging by the markings on the map table the D-Day landings are just beginning.*

would allow the fighters to stay on the ground until 'scrambled' against a specific enemy force. Fortunately, by 1939, British scientists had perfected just such a method, known by the palindrome 'radar' [RAdio Direction And Ranging). Experiments had begun as early as 1934 when, in response to a rather desperate plea from the Air Ministry, scientists at the Radio Research Station, Slough, had rejected the idea of a 'death ray' produced by high-frequency radio beams. Instead, they had suggested the possibility of locating rather than destroying aircraft, using the relatively simple procedure of creating a beam which would be disrupted as the aircraft flew through it: if this could be monitored, rough estimations of direction and altitude could be made. Robert Watson-Watt, chief scientist at Slough, produced a paper entitled 'Detection and Location of Aircraft by Radio Methods' as early as 12 February 1935 and the Air Ministry, impressed by the potential, authorized immediate research.

This began less than two weeks later, using the British Broadcasting Corporation's powerful short-wave transmitter at Daventry. A beam from there was picked up by a special receiver on board a 'traveling laboratory' (a Morris van) and a Handley Page Heyford

ABOVE: *The site of a 'Low Warning' radar system, somewhere in England, 1944. The 'Chain Home' system achieved its object of providing warning of incoming bombers, but by 1941 the Germans had realized that low-level 'intruder' operations, carried out by single fighter-bombers flying at extremely low altitude, could avoid existing radar cover. In response, the British developed 'Low Warning' sets, specially designed to catch the intruder aircraft. As the photograph implies, these were small and highly mobile, comprising a radar system which could be carried in the back of a 3-ton truck: easy and quick to set up, they could be deployed to cover likely areas of attack. After the D-Day landings in June 1944, such systems were sent to join the front-line forces in Europe, where they proved useful in warning of surprise air attack. However, the problem of distinguishing between the aircraft and ground 'clutter' remained: it has still to be completely solved.*

RIGHT: *The interior of a 'Low Warning' system. The operator is listening for interruptions to a beamed signal and is rotating the outside 'dish' by means of the handle on the left. Such work, although often tedious and invariably nonproductive, was vital to the defense of friendly airspace.*

bomber was flown on an interception course. As it crossed the beam, a green spot on an oscilloscope in the van moved vertically to denote interception, and horizontally to denote direction. Watson-Watt then took the experiments further, using pulses of radio energy rather than a continuous beam, the idea being that if the transmitter shut down between pulses, it could act as a receiver for any that might be reflected by a passing aircraft. This had the advantage of locating transmitter and receiver together and enabled far more accuracy at longer range to be achieved, so increasing the warning time available. By May 1937, when the first of these radar stations was established at Bawdsey Manor near Felixstowe on the east coast, it was possible to locate an aircraft flying at 1525m (5000ft) at a range of 64km (40 miles); if the same aircraft approached at 16,675m (35,000ft), the range increased to an impressive 225km (140 miles).

The potential was obvious and, by September 1939, a number of linked stations known as the 'Chain Home' network had been established, supplemented by smaller stations ('Chain Home Low') which operated on shorter radio wavelengths and specialized in tracking low-flying aircraft. Once the information had been gained, it was passed on to fighter control centers, situated in precise sectors of the air-defense system, and, as the incoming bombers were tracked on a special map, a fighter controller called up the interceptor squadrons, giving them precise and accurate details of altitude, direction and range. It was an impressive and effective system and one which, during the Battle of Britain in the summer of 1940, represented the difference between destruction and survival for the British people.

LEFT: *A radar-assisted searchlight, mounted on tracks for ease of movement. Although not in general usage, devices such as this had been developed by British scientists by 1944.*

RIGHT: *A woman factory worker manufactures aluminum foil which will be cut up to make 'Window' (now called 'Chaff'). By 1942, scientists had realized that small strips of foil, cut to match the wavelength of enemy radars, would create such a cloud on the radar screen that tracking would be impossible.*

BELOW: *A Boeing B-17 Flying Fortress, in service with RAF Coastal Command, displays radar aerials in the nose and beneath the wing, used for tracking enemy submarines.*

BELOW RIGHT: *The radar array on the nose of a Messerschmitt Bf-110 night-fighter, 1945. Designed to enable the fighter to approach close to an enemy bomber at night, the system – known as Lichtenstein – was effective.*

NAVAL AVIATION

The Beginnings of Naval Aviation
The Short 184

By 1918, most of the roles of aircraft in a naval context had been laid down. Experiments had been conducted in the difficult art of launching and recovering wheeled aircraft on board flat-decked carriers, and floatplanes had been used for observation, gunfire spotting, torpedo attack and bombing. The age of the aircraft carrier as a central feature of rival fleets may still have been in the future, but much of the preliminary work had been done, based in large measure upon the pioneering spirit of a small group of naval officers and aircraft manufacturers in Britain.

The experiments began in 1911, when Captain Murray F Sueter and Lieutenant D H Hyde-Thomson of the Royal Navy tackled the problem of using aircraft to carry and launch torpedoes. Their main difficulty was one of weight, for by the time that a 408kg (900lb) torpedo had been slung beneath an aircraft already containing two men (pilot and observer), existing engines could not cope, particularly as, in the absence of carriers, the only aircraft available for naval support at sea were floatplanes which required considerable power to take off. In the summer of 1914, the aircraft designer Horace Short was asked to find a solution to the problem. Within a matter of months, he had produced the Short 184, a single-engine floatplane of conventional, if somewhat unassuming, design. Fitted with large wooden floats beneath the central fuselage, as well as smaller ones under the tail and each wing-tip, the 184 was powered by a 225hp Sunbeam Mohawk engine and, in experiments held in early 1915, it proved able to lift the required weight. Government contracts were immediately awarded to several manufacturers to produce further examples, and by the middle of the year the Royal Naval Air Service (RNAS) had been provided with a 'workhorse,' capable of absorbing a number of modifications designed to fit it for new or experimental roles.

LEFT: *Short 184s of the Royal Naval Air Service bomb a Turkish railway junction at El-Afuleh, 1916. Operating from HMS* Empress, *these are standard 184s, with high-fitted radiators/exhausts. From the painting by C R Fleming-Williams.*
BELOW: *A Sopwith 1½ Strutter takes off from a launch platform mounted on a gun turret of a British battleship.*

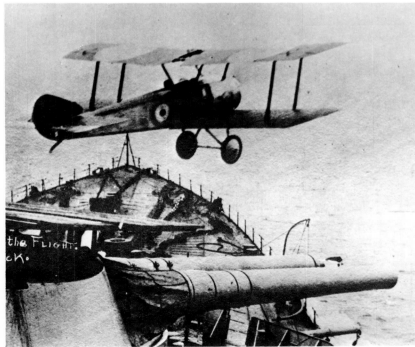

RIGHT: *A Short 184 seaplane lands in calm waters, 1918. The lack of top-mounted radiator identifies this as an 'Improved' type: it is carrying two 50kg (110lb) bombs beneath the fuselage.*

FAR RIGHT: *A Fairey Flycatcher seaplane flies over Grand Harbor, Valetta, Malta, 1928. Used as a carrier-borne or amphibian fighter, the Flycatcher equipped Fleet Air Arm squadrons from 1923 to 1934.*

BELOW: *A late example of a Short 184 is prepared for launch. The much improved engine, with curving exhausts and self-contained radiator, may be seen.*

In fact, torpedo-carrying versions of the 184 proved disappointing, for although they were clearly capable of taking to the air, a number of practical problems arose. Like all floatplanes of the time, the 184 required 'ideal' conditions – a large expanse of calm water, with no strong winds – which were rarely experienced, particularly out at sea. In addition, the weight of the torpedo inevitably cut down the amount of fuel that could be carried, and this restricted both range and operating altitude. Thus, although two of the prototype 184s traveled to the eastern Mediterranean aboard the seaplane tender *Ben-My-Chree* in May 1915 and even managed to attack Turkish supply vessels around the Dardanelles, their inability to travel faster than 120km/h (75mph) or higher than 224m (800ft) left them extremely vulnerable, particularly as the natural heat of the area often led to water in the engine cooling system boiling away. Local modifications were made, but the consensus was that, as a torpedo-carrier, the 184 was not satisfactory.

The aircraft did have other roles to play, however, the most notable of which was naval observation. In the more temperate climate of home waters, performance figures improved, and when the British and German fleets clashed at Jutland in late May 1916, at

least one 184 from the tender *Engadine* carried out a useful reconnaissance patrol, sending back information using a rudimentary wireless set. By 1918, 184s had been deployed aboard a number of tenders for use at sea, while others had become standard issue to naval air stations around the coasts of Britain. In the latter context, they proved particularly valuable for antisubmarine work, searching out and, if possible, attacking German U-boats as they recharged batteries on the surface. Again, practical problems existed – in many cases, the submarines could crash-dive before the slow-moving 184 reached an attack position – but a number of U-boats were spotted and, on at least one occasion, a successful sinking was claimed. Indeed, between 1 May and 12 November 1918, a total of 17,558 hours of antisubmarine patrols were flown, principally in 184s, around the shores of Britain. By then, as a final experiment, 184s had been successfully launched from the deck of the carrier HMS *Furious*, the floats being mounted on a wheeled dolly which was then discarded. These experiments were of less significance than those carried out at the same time using wheeled aircraft such as the Sopwith F-1 Camel, but they were part of a pattern of adaptation and experimentation which ensured the future development of naval aviation.

Short 184 (Mohawk engine)

Type: Single-engine naval floatplane.
Performance: Max speed 120km/h (75mph).
Service ceiling (home waters) 610m (2000ft); (Mediterranean) 224m (800ft).
Endurance 4-5 hours.
Armament: One 355mm (14in) torpedo or 4 × 29kg (65lb) bombs.

ABOVE: *HMS* Argus, *Britain's first flush-deck aircraft carrier, photographed in her special disruptive pattern camouflage, 1918. Taking the hull of the half-completed Italian liner* Conte Rosso, *a flat deck was added to create* Argus *in 1917, although she was commissioned too late to see service in World War I.*

BELOW: *HMS* Hermes, *the first purpose-built aircraft carrier. Laid down in 1918,* Hermes *was not completed in time to see service in World War I and did not join the Fleet until 1923.*

RIGHT: *A German seaplane lands close to a U-boat in coastal waters to deliver a message. The potential for communications at sea using such aircraft was obvious, although in this particular case, the closeness of the shore suggests a training exercise.*

BELOW RIGHT: *The first US Navy aircraft carrier the USS* Langley *in 1927. The* Langley *was converted from a US Navy collier and served with the fleet from 1922 until she was sunk by the Japanese in 1942.*

ABOVE: *A Junkers Ju-87D Stuka dive-bomber on display at a recent air show. This example was captured in Europe in 1945.*

LEFT: *Hawker Hurricane IIC fighters take off from a desert airstrip, North Africa, 1942. These aircraft have been fitted with special 'tropicalized' air filters and each carries four wing-mounted 20mm cannon.*

TOP: *A Messerschmitt Bf-109E-4 of Jagdgeschwader 27 in flight over the Mediterranean, 1942. This aircraft clearly displays the emblem of JG.27 on the nose and the white belly-band which was a characteristic of Luftwaffe aircraft in North Africa.*

between aircraft and ground and naval forces, and in the air between the attack and defense, however, was fiercely disputed, and itself evolved under pressure exerted by technological developments. Indeed, the pace of such change quickened appreciably in the two or three years before the outbreak of war with the introduction of monoplanes into front-line service. Nevertheless, by September 1939 air power had developed along four separate, but intimately related, paths: as the means of providing close support for ground forces; as the means of carrying the offensive to an enemy homeland in the form of strategic bombing; as the means of providing defense against enemy offensive action; and as the means of providing close support for naval forces.

The course, nature and pace of the war in Europe between 1939 and 1942 was determined by Germany, in part because of her central geographical position and in part because she had more accurately gauged the existing balance between the offensive and the defensive in large-scale operations than her various enemies. She had achieved the latter by developing a concept of offensive, mobile firepower provided by an all-arms battle group – armor, motorized infantry, towed artillery and assault engineers – that afforded air power a crucial role in providing close air support for ground forces. The key to this *blitzkrieg* concept was the use of light bombers against both enemy front-line positions and lines of communication, the emphasis of German air operations in this period being directed against enemy rear areas. By concentrating against an enemy's ability to effect a timely reinforcement of a threatened sector or to move fresh forces to seal a breach, German air power was able to help restore to the battlefield a mobility that had been conspicuously lacking in World War I. But in devising a form of warfare that in large measure owed its success to air power's effectiveness in paralyzing an enemy command and control system, Germany possessed neither a patent nor the resources that allowed her both to increase and diversify production to meet new needs. Thus after the fall of France in June 1940 she was to encounter two problems that were to contribute substantially to her final defeat. First, apart from the Balkan campaign in 1941, after June 1940 the only land campaigns Germany fought were against enemies larger, more populous and, in military and industrial terms, more powerful than herself. These powers in their turn developed tactical air forces and introduced into service aircraft of greatly superior performance to those that had paved the way for Germany's earlier, easier victories. Thus the early supremacy of the Ju-87 Stuka was usurped by such aircraft as the Il-2 Sturmovik on the Eastern Front and the P-47 Thunderbolt and Hawker Typhoon in northwest Europe and the Mediterranean theater.

The second problem that Germany faced after 1940 was that an air force that had been developed for intervention over the battlefield could not be endowed with a strategic bombing role, which was needed if her last remaining enemy in 1940, Britain, was to be forced into submission. Moreover, German difficulties were compounded by the fact that by 1940 the technology that had seemed to bestow so many advantages to the offensive had in reality proved even-handed. Developments which had seen two- and four-engine bombers fly faster, higher and to greater ranges than contemporary biplanes also resulted, in time, in monoplane fighters which were good stable gun platforms, and both faster and more maneuverable than bombers. In addition, the development of radar and improved radio communications provided the means of conducting effective defense, and in the course of the Battle of Britain in 1940 the German air force suffered such losses in the course of its daylight raids on military targets that it was forced to switch to night attacks on cities. Subsequently, the RAF suffered exactly the same experience when in its turn it sought to carry the offensive to the enemy homeland. Such was the state of the art before 1944 that bomber forces could not hope to achieve significant results by bombing or at the same time avoid prohibitive losses in the course of daylight raids. It was left to the United States, after October 1943, to demonstrate that such raids were practical, and this she was able to do through a combination of three factors: massive numbers of bombers; the careful devising of formation flying that ensured maximum mutual protection on the part of attacking bombers; and the development of long-range fighter escorts.

It was the appearance over Germany of the latter, particularly the P-51 Mustang and P-38 Lightning, that after 1943 paved the way for the increasingly effective bombing of Germany by the Western Allies. By April 1945 strategic bombing had reduced much of urban Germany to rubble, had all but wrecked Germany's transport systems, and had brought industry to a halt. In terms of its justifying the resources and losses that went into this effort, strategic bombing was a success – but its success coincided with the total collapse of Germany as a result of concurrent defeat on land, at sea and in the air. Inevitably, the defeat on land obscured both the fact and nature of air power's achievement. There was, however, no such obscuring of air power's achievement in the Far East, where American strategic bombing in fair measure destroyed Japan's capacity to wage war by July 1945 and was critically important in bringing about her surrender in the following month.

The American strategic air offensive against Japan – conducted alone by the B-29 Superfortress – effectively lasted no more than five months and owed its success to the peculiarities of geography

RIGHT: *Avro Lancaster B-III of No 619 Squadron, RAF Bomber Command, photographed in February 1944. Issued to the squadron in December 1943, when it was stationed at Woodhall Spa, this aircraft went on to participate in a number of raids over Germany during the latter stages of the 'Battle of Berlin.' On 30 March 1944, it flew from 619's new base at Coningsby on the ill-fated Nuremberg raid, during which it was hit by anti-aircraft fire, losing two of its engines. The pilot managed to nurse the aircraft back to Woodbridge, where it crash-landed and burst into flame. It was completely destroyed. 619 Squadron, formed in April 1943 as a heavy bomber unit, was disbanded in July 1945.*

and urban development that rendered Japanese cities and industry extremely vulnerable to attack from the air. But American strategic bombers had only been able to bring Japan under telling bombardment as a result of advances across the Pacific that had enabled the capture of the Mariana Islands – whence Superfortresses operated after November 1944. These islands, and indeed all the islands secured by the Americans after 1943, were taken as a direct result of the triumph of air power as applied to the naval environment in the shape of the fast carrier task force.

The first use of massed carrier forces had been by the Japanese in the course of their attack on Pearl Harbor on 7 December 1941, the Americans not equalling the six carriers used on that raid in any operation before November 1943. In the course of 1943 and 1944, however, war was brought to the shores of the Japanese islands by a growing number of fast carriers, and had hostilities continued into 1946 the Allies would have deployed no fewer than 30 fast carriers (with another seven in reserve) off the Japanese homeland – all but one of the American and both of the British task groups so employed being roughly equal in size to the Japanese force that

BELOW: *B-17F Flying Fortress bombers of the 390th Bomb Group, Eighth US Army Air Force, plough toward their target in daylight, 1943. The close formation of the Group was designed to provide mutual protection from enemy fighters, the contrails of which may be seen arching away in the background.*

had raided Hawaii five years before. But the effective use of carriers in a strategically offensive role ran in tandem with a switch of emphasis from attack aircraft to fighters within individual air groups. At the start of the Pacific War an American and Japanese carrier, given the task to seek out and destroy enemy main force units, deployed no more than one fighter squadron to one or two squadrons of dive-bombers and one torpedo-bomber squadron. Very quickly, however, both navies discovered the need to deploy extra fighters, if necessary at the expense of striking power, and by 1945, as American carriers were subjected to massed suicide

RIGHT: *A Gloster Gladiator single-seat biplane fighter of the RAF, photographed in 1986. The Gladiator – the last biplane fighter to see service in the RAF – was first flown in September 1934, entering squadron service, with No 72 Squadron, in February 1937. Although obsolete by 1939, examples of the aircraft were involved in the early campaigns of World War II, in Norway, the defense of Malta and in Greece and the Middle East.*

BELOW: *North American P-51D Mustang fighters of the US 23rd Fighter Group line up on an airfield in China, 1945. The P-51D, with its distinctive 'bubble' canopy, was a vast improvement on earlier designs, affording excellent pilot visibility and a good turn of speed – up to 704km/h (437mph) in level flight. By 1945, the D model was equipping a large number of USAAF and RAF squadrons in both the Pacific and European theaters. It was arguably one of the finest fighter aircraft of the war years, outclassing most of its Axis counterparts.*

attack when they operated off the Philippines and Japan, fighters outnumbered bombers by three to one in American fleet units. In part the decline in the number of bombers embarked in an individual carrier was compensated by the growth of the carrier fleet, in part by the introduction into service of high-performance aircraft that could operate in both the fighter and the fighter-bomber roles. But as Allied carrier forces fought their way into the western Pacific, their priority was to secure air supremacy; tactical strikes, in support of forces ashore, was the task increasingly entrusted to land-based and escort carrier air groups.

The Allied plans for the invasion of Japan envisaged the employment of about 100 such escort groups in three roles: ferrying replacement aircraft from rear bases to the fast carriers; providing tactical air support; and antisubmarine attack. It was in the latter role that these ubiquitous ships had already contributed immensely to Allied success in the Battle of the Atlantic, though the number of German submarines their air groups sank were few. Their achievement had been in securing control of the sea around

a convoy, either deterring an enemy attack or guiding surface escorts to their prey. The vast majority of the 352 German submarines sunk by direct attack from the air during the war were destroyed by land-based aircraft and amphibians, in particular by the Liberator, Sunderland and Catalina. In total, aircraft contributed directly or indirectly to the destruction of 416 of the total of 784 German submarines lost between 1939 and 1945, and of the 15 largest German warships sunk or damaged beyond repair in the course of the hostilities, aircraft accounted for nine and shared one with surface warships. Only two major German units were sunk as a result of surface action, and in the Pacific the statistics were much the same: of the total of 70 Japanese carriers, battleships and cruisers sunk between 1941 and 1945, 39 were destroyed by air attack and one was shared between aircraft and warships. Both in the Atlantic and Pacific, Allied naval victories rested on air power, and if the impact of air power at sea was more easily identifiable than its impact on continental warfare, by 1945 it was clear that in both the military and the naval contexts air power had come of age.

RIGHT: *A German V-1 flying bomb, its fuel exhausted, drops toward a target in London, July 1944. The existence of Hitler's 'Vengeance Weapons' had been known to the British since 1942 and a variety of air attacks had been carried out against the factories and launch-sites, but this did not prevent them from being used in 1944.*

BELOW: *A Republic P-47D Thunderbolt fighter is prepared for a mission, 1944. The size of the aircraft may be seen, particularly in terms of its Pratt & Whitney Double Wasp 18-cylinder engine and four-bladed propeller.*

GROUND SUPPORT

ABOVE: *A Junkers Ju-87R-2 of* Stukageschwader *(Dive-Bomber Group)
1 flies over Sicily in May 1941. The 'R' suffix denoted* Reichweite *(Range),
this particular model of the Stuka being fitted with extra fuel tanks in
each wing-root.*

BELOW: *A remarkable series of photographs depicting Ju-87 Stukas
peeling off on a dive-bombing attack, 1942.*

Aircraft in Blitzkrieg
The Junkers Ju-87 Stuka

The overwhelming victories of German arms in the first two years of World War II owed much to the effectiveness of the Luftwaffe in general and of one aircraft, the Junkers Ju-87 Stuka, in particular. Devastating in that it could accurately bomb enemy positions within yards of friendly ground forces, the Stuka was the spearhead of German operations in Poland in 1939, in the West in 1940, and in the Balkans and on the Eastern Front in 1941. Indeed, such was the reputation of the Stuka at this stage of the war that its image and the very word *blitzkrieg* were and have remained to this day virtually synonymous.

The origins of the Stuka were somewhat controversial. The design specifications, issued in 1935, were given at a time when the Luftwaffe as a whole was unconvinced by the claims of dive-bombing and in a way that strongly favored a private venture then being undertaken by Junkers. It owed its acceptance into service to the strong personal influence of Ernst Udet, director of aircraft

BELOW: *Hans-Ulrich Rudel, the greatest Stuka 'ace' of them all. Specializing in aerial tank-busting, he operated on the Eastern Front, where he is credited with destroying 519 Soviet tanks.*

LEFT: *Junkers Ju-87Bs of Stukageschwader 77, photographed at Breslau in August 1937. The aircraft nearest the camera, resplendent in its 'shark's teeth' nose marking, is about to be loaded with a 454 kg (1000 lb) bomb.*

BELOW LEFT: *Mechanics work on the huge 37mm Flak 18 antitank gun under the port wing of a Ju-87G, Eastern Front, 1943. The existence of two of these weapons (one under each wing) gave the Stuka a new lease of life, but it did nothing to improve speed or maneuverability, leaving the aircraft vulnerable to attack.*

procurement, who in 1936 managed to write off its only serious rival, Heinkel's much-superior He-118, in somewhat suspicious circumstances. Be that as it may, the Ju-87A entered production in 1936 and service in 1937, making its operational debut in Spain toward the end of that year.

The Ju-87A was quickly followed into production by the much-improved Ju-87B. With a 1200hp engine in the place of the 640hp engine mounted in the Ju-87, the Ju-87B was faster and able to carry a greater bomber-load than its predecessor. It was also a considerable structural and aerodynamic improvement over the Ju-87A, the latter having been relegated to training duties by the time of the outbreak of war. It was the 'B' variant, therefore, that earned the Stuka its awesome reputation among civilians and army alike in 1939 and 1940. With its sinister, inverted gull wing and fixed undercarriage which gave it a decidedly predatory appearance, the Ju-87Bs lost just 31 of their number in leading the way into Poland and just 14 of their establishment as they led the armored columns to and beyond the Meuse River within five days of the start of the campaign in the West in 1940.

RIGHT: *A group of Ju-87Bs flies in formation, probably prewar. In action, such a group would approach their target and then peel off to attack it in succession, screaming down to drop bombs on ground units or installations.*

BELOW: *A Ju-87G prepares for take-off, Eastern Front, 1943. The twin 37mm antitank cannon may be seen to good effect. It was this particular model of the Stuka that was flown by Hans-Ulrich Rudel in 1943-45, when he achieved fame as a tank-busting 'ace': the impact of the cannon was devastating.*

RIGHT: *A Luftwaffe armorer refills the magazine of an underwing 37mm antitank gun on a Ju-87G, Eastern Front, 1943. The size of the ammunition may be appreciated.*

BELOW RIGHT: *A Ju-87B returns from the attack, its center-line bomb cradle and underwing hard-points empty. This photograph was probably taken over France during the remarkable Blitzkrieg campaign of May-June 1940, when the Stukas played a vital role in the demoralization of Allied ground units. Within a matter of weeks, when the same aircraft encountered the fighters of the RAF over England, the story was different.*

BELOW: *Ju-87B-2 Stukas, probably belonging to Stukageschwader 3, fly toward Tobruk, 1941. Without escort fighters, the Stuka was a vulnerable aircraft, slowed down by its exterior bomb-load and fixed undercarriage.*

The fact that in these early campaigns of the war the Stuka won an almost legendary fame at such trifling cost and at a time when its front-line strength was very small – less than 350 in September 1939 – is witness to the fact that its impact was as much psychological as physical. Used with its screaming sirens against untried troops and civilian refugees, it was as much an instrument of terror as a weapon of war. Its effectiveness in either or both roles, however, depended upon German fighters having secured air supremacy. Slow by contemporary standards and not particularly maneuverable, the Stuka was vulnerable to a determined enemy fighter, and over southern England the Stuka suffered such prohibitive losses that it had to be withdrawn from operations in mid-August 1940, some four weeks before the Battle of Britain reached its climax.

The Stuka was able to regain much of its lost reputation in 1941 in the Mediterranean, where it heavily damaged the carriers HMS *Illustrious* and HMS *Formidable* and sank a number of cruisers and destroyers off Crete, and in the Balkans and Russia. But despite its success and the appearance of the new Ju-87D, which had a 1410hp engine, considerable armor protection and the ability to lift a 1802kg (3968lb) bomb-load, output of Stukas fell in 1941 to 476, a decline of 125 from the previous year. But instead of the Germans phasing the Stuka out of production as was their intention, the lack of any replacement aircraft forced them to resume and expand its program, thereby ensuring that 70 percent of the 5709 Stukas built in the course of the war were built after its obsolescence was

acknowledged. Indeed, the longer the war lasted and the more pronounced enemy air superiority became, the more precarious the Stuka's existence. It continued to see service in its intended role after 1941 and was even pressed into service as a diving fighter against enemy bomber formations, but only on the Eastern Front did it continue to be used to any real effect. There, where the Luftwaffe could often regain a local if temporary supremacy, the Ju-87G proved very effective in a close support role. Equipped with two 37mm (1.5in) cannon, each with six armor-piercing rounds, the Ju-87D was used in an antitank role, but after 1943 it could do no more than cover the withdrawal of depleted and outnumbered Axis formations and try to slow the enemy's advance. Largely replaced in service by Fw-190 fighter-bombers, Stuka production ended in September 1944, although examples were still being flown in 1945, as the Allies closed in on the Reich.

Junkers Ju-87B-1

Type: Single-engine dive-bomber.
Performance: Max speed 349km/h (217mph).
Service ceiling 8000m (26,248ft).
Range 550km (342 miles).
Armament: Three 7.92mm (0.303in) machine-guns; one 454kg (1000lb), four 55kg (110lb) bombs.

Ground-Support in the East
The Ilyushin Il-2 Sturmovik

The estrangement of the Western powers and the Soviet Union after 1945 and the onset of the Cold War in the late 1940s, ensured that Western history of World War II has seldom acknowledged the magnitude of the Soviet achievement and sacrifice in 'The Great Patriotic War.' As a result, relatively little is known about the war on the Eastern Front, and probably no more than two or three Soviet aircraft of the period are known, if only by name, to the public of the Soviet Union's wartime allies. In some ways the latter is not altogether surprising, given the fact that very few Soviet aircraft were of a quality that made them significant in terms of aeronautical development, but the fact remains that probably the most extensively used aircraft of the war, and one which was probably built in greater numbers than any other aircraft in history, is largely unknown in the West.

The Il-2 Sturmovik was developed in the late 1930s in two forms, first as a two-seater *bronirovannyi shtormovik*, an armored assault aircraft, and then in the single-seater layout that entered production and was accepted into service in March 1941. Its progress from drawing board to airfield was difficult, most of its problems being caused by the prototype CKB-57 single-seater being underpowered and having to wait until October 1940 for the delivery of a satisfactory 1680hp liquid-cooled engine. Installed in the place of the original 1370hp powerplant, the new AM-38 engine gave life to an aircraft with no direct counterpart in any other air force at that time and which combined a number of almost contradictory requirements while still remaining a typical piece of Soviet military engineering. Cheap and easy to build and capable of operating from barely prepared grass runways, the Il-2 Sturmovik was

ABOVE: *By 1943, the Sturmovik had been considerably improved, incorporating an extra seat for the gunner, responsible for providing rear protection. Thus, when ground targets were engaged, as here during the Battle of Kursk (July 1943), a watch could be kept for enemy fighters.*

LEFT: *Ilyushin Il-2 Sturmovik ground-support aircraft fly over the forests and frozen lands of western Russia during the winter of 1941-42. These are probably single-seat Il-2s which, although effective against German armor, were vulnerable to interception, particularly because of the lack of rear-facing armament.*

RIGHT: *Il-2m3 Sturmoviks fly over the ruins of Berlin, May 1945. Each aircraft is armed with two VJa 23mm cannon and ShKas 7.62mm machine-guns in the wings, and a single 12.7mm BS machine-gun in the rear cockpit.*

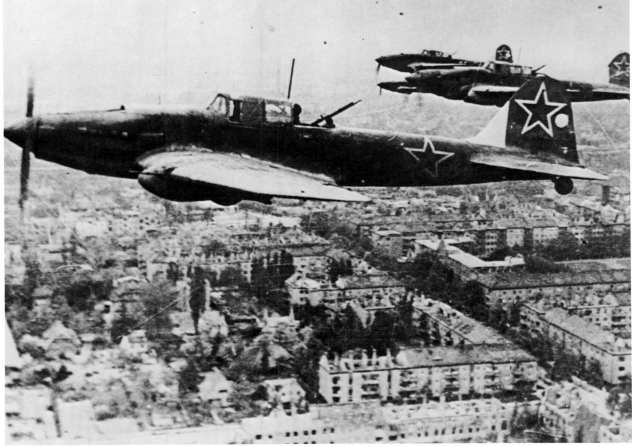

intended for close-support operations. For this role it needed and was provided with a good low-level performance, the best operational altitude being set at 610m (2000ft), reasonable speed and powers of maneuver, and a heavy offensive armament. Moreover, it had to be small, but its most remarkable feature was both the nature and extent of its armor protection. The whole of the cockpit, engine and cooler system was contained within a single, one-piece armored cradle. Abandoning the usual practice of incorporating armor by adding it to the airframe, the Ilyushin design employed the armor of the Sturmovik as the forward fuselage. By this means, the Soviets were able to work 700kg (1540lb) of armor into an aircraft (the Il-2) which, when empty, weighed only 3800kg (8370lb), a defensive ratio unequalled by any other aircraft.

The Sturmovik was to need such protection in the war it was called upon to fight after June 1941, but combat in the first disastrous

months, when it was forced to operate under conditions of overwhelming enemy superiority, quickly showed that while it was well protected against light flak, its lack of a rear gunner made it very vulnerable to enemy fighters. As a result in early 1942, when Sturmovik production was getting into its stride after the forced evacuation of industry to the east, the decision was taken to redesign the cockpit in order to accommodate a rear gunner and to make various other changes of detail. The armored cradle was thus correspondingly lengthened to include a second crew member and the canopy, complete with its 12.7mm (0.5in) machine-gun position, was reshaped to improve aerodynamic qualities. Engine performance was also boosted and the 20mm (0.8in) cannon were replaced by 23mm (0.9in) versions. Thus modified, the new Sturmovik, the Il-2m3, began to enter service in August 1942.

Various other changes were to be effected before production

ABOVE: *An Ilyushin Il-2m3 in flight over the Soviet Union. This is a standard model, displaying all the distinctive characteristics of the design. The cockpit compartment, with its pilot and gunner positions, was literally an armored shell, affording remarkable protection against all but a direct hit: Sturmoviks were renowned for their ability to sustain damage and survive. Cannon and machine-gun positions may be seen on the wings and in the rear cockpit, while empty underwing bomb-racks suggest that the aircraft is returning from a mission.*

RIGHT: *A Sturmovik is prepared for action: as a fuel truck refills the tanks, the mechanics reload the underwing machine-guns. The lack of facilities suggests a forward airstrip, where the 'turn-round' time between missions could be quite remarkable, thereby enabling the Sturmoviks to appear over enemy positions in quick succession, in what was known as the 'Circle of Death.'*

ABOVE: *A Soviet biplane, used for carrying messages and 'spotting' for ground forces, flies over a formation of T-34 tanks as they advance toward Japanese positions in the brief campaign in Manchuria, August-September 1945.*

RIGHT AND BELOW RIGHT: *Petlyakov Pe-2 ground-support machines fly in formation over the Eastern Front. The Pe-2, designed initially as a high-altitude fighter, was transferred to ground attack in 1941. Powered by two Klimov M-105R in-line engines, it had a top speed of 541km/h (336mph) and could carry a useful bomb-load of 998kg (2200lb).*

of the Sturmovik ended in June 1944. Of these, two were structural, later versions being of all-metal construction and fitted with double armored bulkheads, the first three versions of the Il-2 being of metal and wooden construction and without such longitudinal protection. Most of the changes, however, concerned armament. In the place of the early 20mm (0.8in) and 23mm (0.9in) cannon came 37mm (1.5in) antitank cannon and provision for 132mm (5.2in) rockets instead of the earlier 82mm (3.2in) rockets. Underwing positions provided space for alternative payloads of six 100kg (220lb) or 200 2.5kg (5.5lb) hollow-charge bombs, the latter being intended for use against armor. In its final form, the Il-2 model 3 (modified) Sturmovik weighed 5179kg (9604lb), of which 950kg (2092lb) was devoted to armor protection. With its semi-retractable undercarriage, the Sturmovik had a boosted 1700hp engine, a top speed of 404km/h (251mph), a maximum ceiling of 6000m (19,500ft), two 37mm (1.5in) cannon, two forward-firing 7.62mm (0.3in) machine-guns and a 12.7mm (0.5in) rear gun, and a payload of either eight rockets or a maximum of 600kg (1320lb) of bombs. Largely invulnerable to ground fire, the Sturmovik proved devastatingly effective in the attack, but lest its potency be identified solely in terms of aircraft characteristics, it should be noted that its effectiveness in no small measure stemmed from the manner and numbers in which it was used. It was committed to battle *en masse*, being operated from forward airfields on a shuttle basis in what was known as the 'Circle of Death': on a single day of operations a regiment of 30 Sturmoviks could put down more than 40 tonnes of bombs on enemy positions and concentrations. Moreover, the Sturmovik was flown in weather that grounded the Luftwaffe, and its normal operational altitude was between 9m and 46m (30ft and 150ft) with damage from the explosion of one's own bombs and

rockets accepted as standard procedure. Perhaps the most sobering aspect of the aircraft was that for all its fearful reputation, the fact that it was probably built in greater numbers than any other aircraft in history almost certainly ensured that it had losses to match.

Ilyushin Il-2m3
Type: Single-engine ground-attack.
Performance: Max speed 404km/h (251mph).
Service ceiling 6000m (19,500ft).
Range 600km (375 miles).
Armament: Two 23mm (0.9in) cannon, two 7.62mm (0.3in) machine-guns; one 12.7mm (0.5in) machine-gun; 600kg (1320lb) bomb-load.

Ground-Support in the West
The Republic P-47 Thunderbolt

World War II witnessed many remarkable achievements in the field of military aviation and the development of many outstanding aircraft. The Republic P-47 Thunderbolt measured up to the most exacting of standards on four counts. First, it was one of the very few aircraft with a full life cycle, from drawing board to operational employment, wholly within the span of World War II. Second, though it began life as a lightweight fighter, it emerged as the biggest single-engine piston-driven fighter of its time, twice the size of the Spitfire, Mustang and Fw-190, as big as the Beaufighter, Beaufort and Lightning, and about the same weight as the Marauder and Mitchell in their unladen state. Third, the Thunderbolt, in its P-47J configuration, was the first piston-driven aircraft to exceed

805km/h (500 mph) in level flight. Fourth, though developed as a fighter, it operated with equal ease as an escort and close-support fighter, in 1945 blasting Japanese aircraft from the skies and German armor off the battlefield with equal facility. Despite an indifferent introduction to battle in 1943, the Republic P-47 Thunderbolt proved to be one of the most impressive combat aircraft of the war.

The Thunderbolt began life in June 1940 when development of two prototype lightweight fighters, the XP-47 and XP-47A, was halted with the realization that neither could be developed in a way that would enable their incorporating the protection and firepower essential to survival and success in European airspace. Set down that month in a design requirement with no weight specifications,

RIGHT: *A Bristol Beaufighter two-seat strike fighter takes off from Malta, 1941. Designed in 1938 as a high-performance long-range fighter, the Beaufighter proved ideal for adaptation to night-fighting and strike duties. First issued to front-line squadrons in September 1940, it was subsequently modified to carry air-interception radars and a variety of attack weapons, the latter including (in the Mark VIF) four 20mm cannon in the nose and six 0.303in machine-guns in the wings. Provision could also be made for torpedoes, bombs or underwing rockets.*

BELOW: *A Republic P-47D Thunderbolt prepares for take-off: this example retains the original sliding hood, replaced in later versions by the 'bubble' canopy. A B-17 is in the background.*

ABOVE: *A P-47, shown in its prewar colors, is prepared for take-off on a snow-covered field, 1941. Although the huge engine produced design problems, the results were impressive: the P-47 had a top speed of 687km/h (427mph) and, with drop tanks added, could provide bomber escort over a long range.*

the P-47B flew for the first time in May 1941, the first production aircraft coming off the assembly line in March 1942 and entering service in June. In its initial form the Thunderbolt had a 2000hp radial engine, a top speed of 690km/h (429mph) at 8235m (27,000ft), eight 12.6mm (0.5in) machine-guns, and a telescopic undercarriage. The latter was made necessary by the need for a strut high enough to raise the 4.3m (12ft 2in) propeller clear of the ground but short enough to be accommodated between fuselage and gun positions. With a range of just 885km (550 miles), however, the limitations of the P-47B were realized long before the United States entered the war. As a result, the P-47C was lengthened by 266mm (10.5in) in order to allow it to carry a drop tank. This mark was quickly followed into production by the P-47D which showed very little improvement over its predecessor despite being equipped with a more powerful 2300hp engine.

Subsequent development, however, provided considerable diversity within this 12,602-strong class and a major qualitative improvement between the low- and high-number serials of this mark. Most were fitted with bubble canopy and reduced fin to provide all-round visibility, but the significant feature of the later P-47Ds was their ability to carry up to three drop tanks, thus allowing them to negotiate the vast distances involved in southwest Pacific operations and to range deeply into Germany. Despite a

RIGHT: *A close-up of the underwing armament of a Republic P-47N Thunderbolt as it takes off on a ground-support mission in northwest Europe, 1945. The bomb is a 500-pounder, and one could be carried under each wing, but of far more impact were the 5in unguided rockets. A total of 10 rockets could be deployed on a single strike mission. Once these were added to the normal armament of eight wing-mounted 0.5in Colt-Browning machine-guns – the firing of which was likened to 'driving a five-ton truck straight at a wall at 60mph' – the effects of an attack by a P-47 could be devastating. Used in all theaters by 1945, the P-47N was perhaps the best ground-attack aircraft to be deployed by the Allies in World War II; it was still in US Air Force service in 1950, at the beginning of the Korean War, by which time its impact had not been lessened. Like all Allied ground-attack aircraft, however, the P-47 emerged from a fighter design, highlighting the lack of prewar thought about the needs of close support: indeed, of all the combatant powers in World War II, it was only the Germans and the Soviets who devoted time to the evolution of specific ground-attack designs.*

relatively poor climb and turn at low and medium altitudes, the Thunderbolts proved effective both as escorts to American bomber formations and in dealing with German low-level intruder raids over Britain. Subsequently the P-47M was developed with a 2800hp engine and a top speed of 761km/h (473mph) in order to deal with V-1 rockets, but though these Thunderbolts never arrived in Britain to deal with this particular enemy, they were able to meet the challenge presented by the Messerschmitt Me-262 and Arado Ar-234 jets. The final wartime Thunderbolt, the P-47N, was the only variant with fuel tanks in its wings, and with a full internal and external fuel load it had a range of 3781km (2350 miles) as a fighter or a range of 1288km (800 miles) with a 908kg (2000lb) bomb-load. Its maximum bomb-load was 1135kg (2500lb).

Effective though it was as a fighter, the Thunderbolt's combination of high speed, good payload and ability to take heavy punishment ensured that it, like the Hawker Typhoon, was used extensively in the close-support role. Initially equipped with anything up to five triple bazooka-type mounts for 114mm (4.5in) rockets, the more usual armament for attack missions was ten 127mm (5in) high-velocity rockets carried on stub, zero-length fittings. Known as 'the Juggernaut,' or more affectionately as 'the Jug,' the

Thunderbolt in its tank-busting role contributed massively to Allied success in the Normandy campaign and thereafter served on the European mainland until the end of the German war. Used in every theater with the single exception of Alaska, the Thunderbolt was supplied to the British, Free French and Soviets, these three Allies being supplied with a combined total of 1479 of the 15,477 that were built. With the final deliveries into service made in September 1945, the Thunderbolt continued in American service until 1955 and with various other armed forces until the early 1960s, earning its keep in a variety of roles, even in the age of the jet.

Republic P-47N Thunderbolt
Type: Single-engine fighter/fighter-bomber.
Performance: Max speed 751km/h (467mph).
Service ceiling 13,115m (43,000ft).
Range 3781km (2350 miles).
Armament: Eight 12.6mm (0.5in) machine-guns; two 454kg (1000lb) and one 227kg (500lb) bomb-load; ten 127mm (5in) rockets.

RIGHT: *A Hawker Tempest II single-seat fighter-bomber shows its clean lines on a test-flight, 1944. Designed for long-range operations in the Far East, the Tempest II arrived in front-line squadrons too late to see action, and was, in fact, one of the last piston-engine fighters to serve in the RAF. Powered by a Bristol Centaurus V or VI radial engine, the aircraft was capable of a top speed of 708km/h (440mph) and was armed with four 20mm cannon in the wings. It also had fixtures for rockets or bombs.*

BELOW: *Hawker Typhoon 1B. Later versions of the Typhoon, characterized by 'bubble' canopies and faired-over cannon, were equipped with underwing points for eight 3in rockets, the use of which was devastating against ground targets, especially in northwest Europe in 1944-45. Field Marshal Erwin Rommel was injured in a Typhoon attack in July 1944.*

THE FIGHTER

The British Fighter
The Supermarine Spitfire

Very occasionally an aircraft evokes an era or embodies a nation at war. The Supermarine Spitfire is such an aircraft. Its name is all but synonymous with British air power in World War II and is forever associated with the period when, with the Hawker Hurricane, the Spitfire stood between Germany and undisputed control of the continent of Europe. The only combat aircraft in the world to be in production in both 1938 and 1947, the Spitfire was the very symbol of Britain at war – in defeat, in isolation and in victory.

Beginning life as a private, non-contract venture in 1934 after Supermarine's Type 224 failed to secure a contract for an RAF fighter that went to the Gloster Gladiator, the Spitfire first flew on 5 March 1936. Described as 'simple and easy to fly and (with) no vices,' the Spitfire was able to register a top speed of 562km/h (349mph), climb to 6100m (20,000ft) in 8 minutes and 20 seconds, and reach a service ceiling of 10,800m (35,400ft). Such was the con-

fidence that the aircraft inspired, the RAF ordered 310 machines before test evaluation was complete. The first Spitfires to enter service did so in August 1938. By the time of Britain's declaration of war on Germany in September 1939, some 400 Spitfires were serving

LEFT: *A Supermarine Spitfire Vb of No 40 Squadron, South African Air Force, flies over the North African coast, 1942.*
RIGHT: *The epitome of Britain's fighter strength in 1940: a Hawker Hurricane and Supermarine Spitfire fly in formation.*
BELOW: *A Supermarine Spitfire of No 303 (Polish) Squadron, RAF Fighter Command shows its lines to the camera high above England, 1941. No 303 Squadron, formed in August 1940, had a distinguished wartime record.*

RIGHT: *Pilots of No 71 Squadron, RAF Fighter Command, 'scramble' toward their waiting Hurricane fighters. No 71 Squadron was formed in September 1940 from American volunteers – for that reason it was known as an 'Eagle' Squadron – but did not fire its guns in anger until the following April. In September 1942, it was transferred to United States command as No 334 Squadron of the 4th Pursuit Group.*

FAR RIGHT: *The formidable nose armament of a British de Havilland Mosquito fighter: four 0.303in machine-guns and a single 20mm cannon. Although rarely used in the role of a pure fighter, the Mosquito had an undeniable ability to survive against most enemy interceptors, using a mix of speed and firepower.*

with Fighter Command, the performance of the aircraft having been improved by the introduction of the controllable airscrew which raised top speed to 594km/h (369mph).

Not committed to the Battle of France in the spring of 1940, the Spitfire had to be content with only the occasional intruder into British airspace until May and June, when it entered the battle over the ports from which Allied troops were being evacuated. Thereafter, it served with 19 of Fighter Command's 52 squadrons during the Battle of Britain, but while the more numerous Hurricane accounted for more enemy aircraft between July and October 1940 than all other types of British aircraft combined, the Spitfire emerged from this as the 'glamour' British aircraft and the one with the greatest development potential of all British fighters. Even before the Battle of Britain drew to a close, the first of nearly 40 development marks that were to enter service, the Mark II, made its appearance with operational squadrons, and it was with this version of the Spitfire that the RAF began in December 1940 to mount offensive operations over enemy-occupied territory. The mainstay

of this effort, however, was the Mark V, which entered service in February 1941. This aircraft, constructed in greater numbers than any other Spitfire variant, was the first Spitfire built as a fighter-bomber and also the first to see service outside northwest Europe.

BELOW: *The Duke of York (soon to be King George VI) inspects the prototype of the Supermarine Spitfire, May 1936. Designed by R J Mitchell, the aircraft first flew on 5 March 1936.*

With each successive mark of Spitfire the British were able to match parallel German improvement of its principal opponent, the Messerschmitt Bf-109, but in the second half of 1941 the Luftwaffe for the first time secured a clear technical and qualitative advantage over the Spitfire with the introduction of the Fw-190, complete with a radial engine that could develop 2100hp. The Spitfire's obvious inferiority to the newcomer prompted a rapid and twofold reaction. To date, development of the Spitfire had taken the form of improvement of an existing airframe and engine, but with the appearance of the Fw-190 such development clearly had limited application. The new Merlin 61 engine, of 1660hp and with a two-speed supercharger, was able to give the new Mark IX a speed of more than 644 km/h (400mph), and as an interim aircraft the Mark IX was to perform very credibly, but in the longer term the only answer to the new generation of German fighters was to rebuild the Spitfire around the larger, more powerful Griffon engine.

Whereas the Mark IX entered service in July 1942 and recorded its first victory against an Fw-190 that same month, the Griffon-powered Mark XII, with an engine that developed 1735hp at only 305m (1000ft), did not enter service until 1943. With a speed of 641km/h (398mph) the Mark XII, along with the Typhoon, proved effective in dealing with the very small-scale, low-altitude raids to

---

Supermarine Spitfire Va

Type: Single-engine fighter/fighter-bomber.
Performance: Max speed 602km/h (374mph).
Service ceiling 11,285m (37,000ft).
Range 1825km (1135 miles).
Armament: Eight 7.92mm (0.303in) machine-guns.

LEFT: *A de Havilland Mosquito fighter-bomber receives its load of 3in rockets. With four of these weapons under each wing, the effects could be awe-inspiring – the equivalent of a broadside from a 10,000-ton cruiser, according to some estimates.*

BELOW, FAR LEFT: *Air Chief Marshal Sir Hugh Dowding, Chief of RAF Fighter Command during the Battle of Britain in 1940. An uncharismatic man, he was nevertheless the chief architect of victory, carefully husbanding his resources and using them skillfully throughout the difficult months of battle. He resigned, unpromoted and largely unrecognized, in 1942.*

RIGHT: *One of the most remarkable photographs of the air war: a Spitfire pilot maneuvers close to a V-1 flying bomb, placing his wing-tip under that of the enemy with the intention of tipping it over. As the V-1 was an unguided weapon, this would send it plummeting to the ground, short of its target.*

BELOW: *A Spitfire XIX, designed (and painted) for high-altitude photo-reconnaissance work. Produced toward the end of World War II, the XIX had a fully pressurized cockpit and a Griffon 66 engine. It could reach a top speed of 740km/h (460mph).*

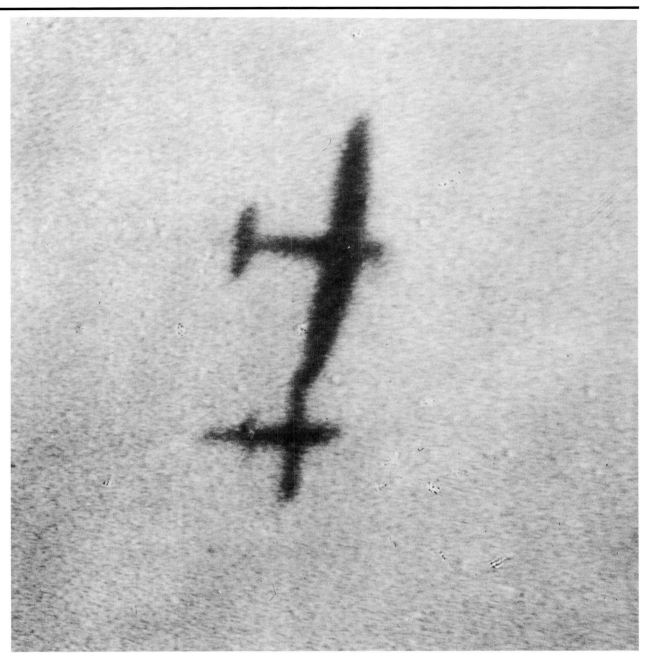

LEFT: *Sir Frank Whittle (right) discusses the finer points of his jet engine with a journalist, 1948. Whittle had first recognized the potential of jet propulsion while a cadet at the RAF College, Cranwell, and in 1930 he registered his provisional specification for a turbojet engine. But the Air Ministry showed little interest, and it was left to Whittle to finance his own development project. On 12 April 1937, his centrifugal flow engine was fired for the first time, and although it still required refinement, its potential was apparent. Even so, it was to take another four years and the pressure of a world war before Whittle received official backing. Without his dedication and brilliance, Britain would have lagged far behind the Germans.*

BELOW: *The diminutive Gloster E28/39 – Britain's first jet-powered aircraft. Developed purely as a test-bed for Frank Whittle's jet engine, the E28/39 took to the air on 15 May 1941. Jerry Sayers, the pilot on that historic occasion, described the aircraft as the easiest he had ever flown.*

which the Luftwaffe had been reduced by this stage of the war, but the Mark XII was quickly supplanted by the Mark XIV. Intended for operations at high altitude, the Mark XIV had a 2050hp Griffon engine, a five-blade airscrew, a two-speed supercharger and intercooler. This gave the Mark XIV a maximum speed of 721km/h (448mph) and the ability to climb to 6100m (20,000ft) in seven minutes, the best performance figures of all wartime Spitfire marks other than those built solely for photographic reconnaissance duties. The various improvements worked into the Mark XIV, however, were only achieved by a considerable increase of weight compared to the Mark XII, by lengthening the nose and, by way of compensation, increasing the wing area. The Mark XIV, therefore, saw a return to the distinctive wing-shape of the early Spitfire – which had been lost with the equally distinctive if unaesthetic clipped wing that had first made its appearance with Mark V variants in an attempt to enhance speed and maneuverability.

While the Merlin and Griffon engines led to parallel development of the Spitfire after 1942, considerations of wing configuration were to weigh heavily in British calculations in a third aspect of Spitfire development and deployment. The massive qualitative improvement of RAF fighters after 1938 had no equivalent in the Fleet Air Arm, and such were the inadequacies of British carrier fighters in the opening phase of the war that in January 1941 the Royal Navy was forced to introduce a 'navalized' Hurricane as the first single-seat monoplane to go to sea in a British carrier. The inferiority of the Sea Hurricane to the latest fighters, plus the problems that beset the development programs of British purposebuilt naval fighters, however, inevitably ensured that the Seafire I entered service with the Royal Navy in June 1942.

The Seafire I was in reality a straight conversion of the Spitfire Mark Vb, but while it and its successor, the Seafire II, represented a considerable improvement over its predecessors, both suffered from two major deficiencies. They were too large for easy stowage in hangars, and it was not until the appearance of the Seafire III, with its curious double-folding wings, that the problems surrounding the handling of Seafires in hangars and on lifts were resolved. Unfortunately, there was little that could be done to remedy the Seafire's other inadequacies with regard to carrier work. The Seafire was too weak to withstand the stresses imposed on undercarriage and fuselage by heavy deck landings and arrester wires, and the Seafires gained a notorious reputation for writing themselves off as 'other operational losses.' Moreover, their lack of range and inability to operate at high altitude imposed severe restrictions upon their tactical employment, but given the British determination not to rely solely upon American naval fighters and the problems that continued to dog the development of the Sea Fury, the Seafire remained in service not just in World War II but during the Korean War (1950-53) as well.

Spitfires and Seafires continued in service until 1954, the last British operational mission being flown on 1 April – the 36th anniversary of the founding of the RAF – by a PR-XIX, a mark which had entered service 10 years earlier as a result of the marrying of a Mark XIV airframe and Mark Vc wing. Such a pedigree, plus the length of time that the aircraft remained in front-line service, were in many ways a remarkable and appropriate tribute to the Spitfire and its makers. In front-line service for a period of 16 years that spanned biplanes and jet aircraft, the Spitfire evolved through perhaps as many as 40 official and unofficial variants, doubled its powerplant and increased its speed by 35 percent and rate of climb by 80 percent between first and last marks, yet never lost its graceful lines and superb aerodynamic qualities. It was to the end a most beautiful aircraft, certain of an enduring reputation.

BELOW: *A Gloster Meteor F-3 single-seat twin-engine jet fighter of No 616 Squadron, RAF Fighter Command, Lübeck, May 1945. The Meteor was the only British jet fighter to see wartime action.*

The American Fighter
The Lockheed P-38 Lightning

Though overshadowed in the ranks of American fighter aircraft of World War II by the Mustang, the Lockheed P-38 Lightning proved a versatile, formidable aircraft in the European and Pacific theaters of operations and was the only American combat aircraft in production both in December 1941 and August 1945.

Ordered in 1937 and first flown in 1939, the Lightning incorporated a startling array of revolutionary innovations within a highly individualistic, distinctive profile. A twin-boom design, two turbo-superchargers, a tricycle landing gear, stainless steel and flush riveting were all combined in an aircraft that was between two

and three times the size of contemporary fighters but which nevertheless was the first aircraft to exceed 644km/h (400mph) in level flight. Its twin-engine layout, moreover, enabled the Lightning to carry a massive concentration of firepower in its relatively small central nacelle, up to eight 12.7mm (0.5in) M-2 machine-guns and 500 rounds per gun being adopted in certain of the later marks. Its great structural stength enabled the Lightning to carry up to 1816kg (4000lb) of ordnance or two 300 US gallon drop tanks on inner-wing pylons, and with a full fuel load all 'G' mark Lightnings and their successors were able to fly the North Atlantic.

LEFT: *A surviving example of the Lockheed P-38 Lightning. First flown in January 1939, the P-38 was a revolutionary design in a number of ways: its twin tail-booms, tricycle undercarriage, turbo-supercharged engines and formidable armament all marked it out as different, while its ability to reach speeds in excess of 644km/h (400mph) put it virtually in a class of its own in 1939.*

BELOW: *A pleasing shot of a P-38 in flight, showing its unique configuration – something which led the Germans to dub the aircraft* Der Gabelschwanz Teufel *('the fork-tailed devil') when they encountered it in the skies of Europe in 1942. The pilot's all-round visibility was an added bonus.*

RIGHT: *P-38 Lightnings in line astern over the Pacific, 1943. It was in this theater that the most dramatic Lightning operation of the war took place when, on 18 April 1943, 16 P-38s of the 339th Squadron flew from Guadalcanal to Bougainville to intercept and shoot down the Japanese aircraft carrying Admiral Isoroku Yamamoto on an inspection tour. The Lightnings appeared spot on time, flying at the extremes of their range: Yamamoto was killed.*

BELOW: *P-38s, fitted with long-range fuel tanks beneath the wings, prepare to carry out bomber escort duties in northwest Europe, 1944. The P-38 was capable of flying to a range of 914km (585 miles) and, armed with one 20mm Hispano cannon and four 0.5in machine-guns in the nose, was a formidable opponent in the air war.*

LEFT: *An early version of the Bell P-39 Airacobra single-seat fighter, photographed in 1940. Designed initially as a company venture, with no official backing, the P-39 was ordered by the French in 1940 and, after the fall of France in June, the contract was taken over by the British. An unorthodox design, with its tricycle undercarriage and engine sited aft of the pilot, the aircraft suffered from a lack of effective range, for although the official figure was 1086km (675 miles), in practice it was nearer 480km (300 miles), even with auxiliary fuel tanks added. Over 5000 P-39s were issued to the Soviets under Lend-Lease.*

This combination of great endurance, high speed, formidable firepower and ruggedness enabled the Lightning to meet the design specifications for a long-range interceptor and escort fighter, and then to perform in these roles in wartime with distinction. It was somewhat ironical, therefore, that when acquired by Britain in 1940 the Lightning was found not to measure up to RAF requirements. Such a state of affairs was the result of Britain's inability to acquire the 12-cylinder liquid-cooled Allison V-1710 engines that powered the aircraft, the C-15 engines with which British Lightnings were equipped proving no substitute for the more advanced American powerplants. In British service, however, the Lightning acquired armor and self-sealing tanks, and when these improvements were grafted onto a high performance product the result was an impressive combat aircraft. The Lightning might have lacked the agility of single-engined contemporaries, but it had a higher ceiling and a superior rate of climb and

dive than such opponents as the Fw-190 – and it could meet the latter in battle over Berlin from bases in the United Kingdom. Moreover, it had the ability, unique among front-line daylight fighters, to survive the loss of an engine, many damaged Lightnings being able to return to base on a single propeller.

The formidable reputation that the Lightning enjoyed by the end of World War II stemmed mainly from its performance as both escort and interceptor. It was long-range Lightnings from

Lockheed P-38L Lightning
Type: Twin-engine fighter.
Performance: Max speed 666km/h (414mph). Service ceiling 13,420m (44,000ft). Range 724km (450 miles).
Armament: One 20mm (0.8in) cannon, four 12.7mm (0.5in) machine-guns.

ABOVE: *Curtiss P-40B Tomahawk fighter of No 112 Squadron, RAF Fighter Command, Sidi Heneish, North Africa, September 1941.*
TOP: *A Northrop P-61 Black Widow night-fighter. Designed in 1941, the P-61 was fitted with SCR-720 air interception radar in the nose, backed by four 20mm belly-mounted cannon.*
LEFT: *North American P-51 escort fighters of the 361st Fighter Group, Eighth USAAF, 1944. Note three different models on show – the nearest aircraft is an early P-51D, without fin strake; that behind it is a later D; in the background is a P-51B.*

Guadalcanal that in April 1943 accounted for the Mitsubishi G4M Betty bomber carrying Admiral Yamamoto (Commander-in-Chief Combined Fleet) over southern Bougainville, and in the course of the Pacific War the Lightning accounted for more Japanese aircraft than any other type of aircraft in Allied service. But in part the Lightning's reputation owed something to the aircraft's ability to operate in a number of operational and noncombat roles. Some Lightnings were fitted with skis in order that they might operate under arctic conditions, and others were adapted to serve as ambulances capable of carrying two stretcher cases. Inevitably, the high speed of the Lightning enabled it to be used on photographic reconnaissance missions, while its central nacelle provided space for electronic countermeasures equipment, an ASH radar and twin cockpits for night-fighting duties, and for a bombardier when Lightnings were used in formations for high-level bombing missions. With the ability to carry bombs, incendiary clusters, smoke canisters or up to 14 102mm (4in) or 127mm (5in) rockets, the Lightning was able to function effectively as a fighter-bomber in all theaters; virtually the only operational role it did not perform was that of a torpedo-bomber, but it had the ability to carry two aerial torpedoes. Such versatility ensured that the Lightning rightly earned its place as one of the most outstanding Allied aircraft to serve during World War II.

The German Fighter
The Focke Wulf Fw-190

The mainstay of the German fighter arm after 1942, the Focke Wulf Fw-190 began life in 1937 with the Luftwaffe requirement for a single-engine fighter to complement the Bf-109 which had first flown in 1935 and which was then in service with General Franco's Nationalist forces in Spain. To meet this requirement, Focke Wulf proposed an aircraft built around either an orthodox, in-line, liquid-cooled Daimler Benz engine or, more radically, a BMW-139 radial engine. Such were the demands on the former, however, that the latter alternative was adopted despite the prevailing prejudice against radial powerplants.

First flown on 1 June 1939, the Fw-190 was slow to get into production and did not reach front-line squadrons for operational testing until June 1941. Its first encounter with RAF fighters did not come until 27 September, but in the months that followed it very quickly demonstrated its clear superiority over the Spitfires then in service with Fighter Command. Some 32-48km/h (20-30mph) faster than the Spitfire Mark V, which it could out-dive and out-turn, the first Fw-190 variants were armed with a powerful array of cannon yet were smaller than their British opponents. It was not until the second half of 1942 that the Fw-190 found its advantages eroded by the Spitfire Mark IX and was forced, thereafter, to give battle on more or less equal terms. In the meantime, however, the Fw-190

had achieved a two-to-one success rate against the Spitfire and had done much to stem the shift in the balance of power in the skies over northwest Europe that had taken place after June 1941 with the German invasion of the Soviet Union.

Like the Spitfire, the Fw-190 evolved through a considerable number of variants and marks, there being no fewer than 28 variants of the Fw-190A alone. In the course of its lifetime, the Fw-190 appeared as a fighter, fighter-bomber and night intruder, but while every aspect of its performance was improved in its remaining years, the Fw-190 was unable to operate effectively in its design role as a fighter and its declining fortune and effectiveness proved a remarkably accurate barometer of German fortunes. The technical superiority of the Fw-190 of 1941 could not be sustained in the

ABOVE: *Adolf Galland, German fighter 'ace' in the Battle of Britain and, from 1941 to 1945, Commander of the Luftwaffe's Fighter Arm. He was officially credited with 103 'kills.'*

LEFT: *A Focke-Wulf Fw-190G-3 of Schlachtgeschwader (Attack Group) 10 over Rumania in 1944. The 'G' series, developed in 1943, took the standard Fw-190 fighter and converted it to fighter-bomber status by deleting all fuselage-mounted weapons, restricting armament to two 20mm MG 151 cannon in the wing-roots, and adding a center-line bomb-rack capable of taking up to 500kg (1102lb) of bombs. The aircraft shown here has clearly carried out an attack mission, its bomb-rack being empty.*

BELOW: *A Focke-Wulf Fw-190A-4 fighter is prepared for take-off, Eastern Front, early 1942. The wing-mounted armament of 20mm MG 151 cannon (in the wing-roots) and 20mm MG FF cannon (on the wing leading edge) may be clearly seen. With two 7.92mm MG 17 machine-guns in the fuselage, the 190A was a formidable machine.*

ABOVE: *A Luftwaffe fighter unit, equipped with Focke-Wulf Fw-190A-5s, prepares for its next sortie, Germany, 1943. The A-5 differed from its predecessors in very minor ways, although it is interesting to note that these particular aircraft seem to have had their 20mm MG FF cannon removed from the wing leading edges – a common occurrence under operational conditions.*

LEFT: *One of the more unusual aircraft of the wartime Luftwaffe: a Dornier Do-335 Pfeil (Arrow). This twin-engine machine operated on the center-line thrust principle, in which one engine drove a propeller in front of the pilot and another drove a pusher screw to the rear. The Do-335 could reach a speed of 763km/h (474mph), but never saw action.*

face of Anglo-American developments, and in any event, after 1942, whatever remained of German technical superiority could not offset a growing enemy superiority of numbers. From 1942 onward the Fw-190, like the whole Luftwaffe and indeed the entire Wehrmacht, found itself over-committed and confronted by too many responsibilities on widely separated fronts to be able to be strong in any particular theater. This was particularly the case on the Eastern Front, where any local Fw-190 superiority was more than offset by a general Soviet superiority over the front as a whole,

Focke Wulf Fw-190A
Type: Single-engine fighter.
Performance: Max speed 652km/h (405mph).
Service ceiling 11,407m (37,400ft).
Range 805km (500 miles).
Armament: Two 13mm (0.51in), four 20mm (0.8in) machine-guns.

RIGHT: *Messerschmitt Bf-109F fighters prepare for a night mission, Germany, 1942. First flown in 1940, the 109F was a considerable improvement on earlier designs, housing the more powerful Daimler Benz 601E engine and carrying an altered armament fit, characterized by the deletion of 20mm MG FF cannon from the wings and the addition of a single 15 or 20mm MG 151 cannon firing through the hollow propeller boss. Although not ideal for night-fighting duties, the 'F' was a useful day-fighter.*

BELOW: *An Italian Fiat CR-42 single-seat biplane fighter of the 95th Squadron, 18th Group of the Regia Aeronautica, captured by the British in 1940 after being shot down during air raids on southern England. The CR-42, first flown as late as January 1939, could only manage a speed of 450km/h (280mph).*

and in northwest Europe, when the Fw-190 was faced by American opposition. Given the fact that the performance of the Fw-190 fell away at altitudes above 6405m (21,000ft). American bombing tactics forced the Fw-190 to give battle under unfavorable conditions, while the appearance of the Lightning, Thunderbolt and Mustang merely added to the difficulties under which it operated.

In order to meet the threat posed by American massed bomber attacks, the Germans produced new marks of Fw-190 and new weapons and tactics. The Fw-190 was equipped with bombs and rockets for use against bomber formations from above, while more conventional firepower was boosted by additional unsynchronized cannon housed under the outer wing. With the Fw-190D, moreover, the Germans once more regained a speed advantage over enemy

fighters, this particular mark being powered by a liquid-cooled engine capable of developing 2240hp for a top speed of 708km/h (440mph). Such improvements and the undoubted courage with which the Fw-190 was flown, however, could not stem the tide of defeat, and it was a measure of the Luftwaffe's decline and the inability of its fighters to withstand the growing pressure exerted by Anglo-American air power that on 6 June 1944 Fw-190 formations in France had been withdrawn to places as far from Normandy as Metz and Rheims – although the only two German aircraft to appear over the invasion beaches on that day were Fw-190s. For all its technical excellence and the fact that some 20,000 Fw-190s were built in the course of World War II, the Fw-190 could not meet the challenge presented by total war.

RIGHT: *Messerschmitt Me 163 Komet rocket-powered fighter, 1944. Fueled by a highly dangerous mixture of* T-Stoff *(hydrogen peroxide) and* C-Stoff *(alcohol/hydrazine), the 163 was not an easy aircraft to fly, but its ability to climb to 4880m (16,000ft) in a minute gave it tremendous potential.*

BELOW RIGHT: *A Messerschmitt Me-262B-1a/U1 jet-engine night-fighter, 1945. First flown in July 1942, the 262 could reach a top speed of 868km/h (540mph). Two-seat trainers were rare – night-fighter variants rarer still.*

ABOVE: *Mitsubishi A6M5* Reisen *fighters (Zeroes or Zekes to the Allies) are readied for take-off at an airfield in Korea, 1945. An aircraft which took the Allies by surprise in 1941, the Zero was designed as a carrier-borne navy fighter, yet proved just as formidable when deployed from land bases. Making its first flight on 1 April 1939, it outclassed most of the Allied fighters in the Far East and Pacific theaters, at least until the introduction of the Grumman F6F Hellcat in 1943. By then, Mitsubishi had already initiated further development, producing the first of the A6M5 versions in August 1943. Faster than previous models – the A6M5 could reach a speed of 660km/h (410mph) – and with increased armament (a mix of 13.2 and 7.7mm machine-guns), the new variant had obvious potential.*

RIGHT: *British and Italian officers and men meet on the airfield at Brindisi soon after the Italian surrender in September 1943. They are standing in front of a Macchi C-202 single-seat fighter, perhaps the best Italian design of the war years. First flown in August 1940, the 202 could achieve a top speed of 590km/h (367mph) and enjoyed good maneuverability and rate of climb. This particular example has had its fascist markings removed.*

BOMBING

The Night Bomber
The Avro Lancaster

By far the most famous and important British heavy bomber of World War II, and qualitatively probably second only to the Boeing B-29 Superfortress in this very exclusive class of aircraft, the Avro Lancaster was curious both in its pedigree and in the fact that during the war it did not undergo any substantial in-service development. The Lancasters in 1945 were almost the same as those that entered service in December 1941, the chief point of difference between the three main production versions that entered service being their engines.

The Lancaster originated in two specifications laid down by the RAF in 1936. Anxious to build up a substantial strike force in the shortest possible time, the RAF sought to acquire both two-engine medium and four-engine heavy bombers, and from the various development programs that were put in hand at this time three aircraft emerged: the Avro Manchester and the four-engine Short Stirling and Handley Page Halifax. The first of these, the Avro

Manchester, proved underpowered and very difficult to fly, not that such weaknesses prevented its entering service in October 1940. But before it did so the decision was taken to replace the troublesome, unreliable twin-Vulture engines of the Manchester with either four separate Merlin engines or two Centaurus or Sabre engines of proven performance and reliability. The latter option was discarded when a suitably modified Manchester B Mark III, with four Rolls-Royce Merlin XX engines, successfully completed its maiden flight on 9 January 1941. On the strength of subsequent service trials, the RAF ordered that the building of Manchesters be

FAR LEFT: *Avro Lancaster 'City of Lincoln,' maintained by the Battle of Britain Memorial Flight and painted in the colors of No 617 Squadron (the Dambusters).*
BELOW: *Avro Lancaster B1 heavy bombers of No 50 Squadron, RAF Bomber Command, based at Swinderby, August 1942. This squadron took part in the low-level raid on Le Creusot in October 1942.*

ended after the 200th delivery and that the Manchester assembly lines be kept open in order to allow subsequent conversion pending full Lancaster production. The first flight by a Lancaster, albeit a converted Manchester, was made on 31 October 1941, service deliveries beginning on Christmas Eve.

The first Lancasters belonged to the most numerous of the seven marks built during World War II, the Mark I. This particular version of the Lancaster showed some diversity, the most notable being the removal of the central fin and ventral turret after the first deliveries. They also showed diversity of powerplant, but while three types of Merlin engine were employed within this single class, the common initial feature was that their engines were British-built. The Mark III series showed a similar diversity of engines, but these were American-built Merlins. The cause of simplicity, however, was not helped by the fact that some Mark I Lancasters

were retrofitted with American engines and by the use of the latter in Canadian-built Mark Is, which were redesignated Mark Xs. The Mark II, however, was equipped with a powerful British radial engine, the Bristol Hercules, but this variant was developed as a precaution against any possible shortfall of American deliveries. When the lack of a need for such insurance was realized, Mark II production was ended with the 300th delivery while production of the Mark I and Mark III reached 3425 and 3039 respectively, Canada contributing a further 430 aircraft. The other Lancaster versions to enter service were the Marks IV and V, both used for development work on the Lincoln program, and the Marks VI and VII. The Mark VI was a conversion from either the Mark I or Mark III, and was used exclusively on electronic countermeasures operations, while the Mark VII had Austin engines and a dorsal turret further forward than other Lancasters.

ABOVE: *A Handley Page Halifax Mark II, Series I four-engine heavy bomber, photographed before issue to a front-line squadron. The original Halifax, developed from a twin-engine design, first flew on 25 October 1939, and production models of the Mark I, characterized by their lack of dorsal turret, entered squadron service, with No 35 Squadron, in late 1940. The Mark II added a two-gun dorsal turret, as shown here.*
BELOW: *A Handley Page Hampden of No 408 (Goose) Squadron, Royal Canadian Air Force, Syerston, August 1941. The Hampden, a prewar design, was poorly suited to the bombing campaign against Germany, lacking range, bomb-load and adequate defensive armament. It was withdrawn in September 1942.*

Avro Lancaster I
Type: Four-engine heavy bomber.
Performance: Max speed 462km/h (287mph).
Service ceiling 7472m (24,500ft).
Range 2671km (1660 miles).
Armament: Eight 7.92mm (0.303in) machine-guns; 6356kg (14,000lb) bomb-load.

ABOVE: *Before and after shots of the Moehne Dam, May 1943.*
TOP: *A close-up of Barnes Wallis' famous 'bouncing bomb,' used by converted Lancasters of No 617 Squadron to hit the Ruhr Dams on 16/17 May 1943. The bomb was launched spinning backward, so it would skip as it hit the water.*

ABOVE: *A Halifax Mark II is made ready for a night-time mission over Germany: 454kg (1000lb) bombs are about to be loaded.*
RIGHT: *227kg (500lb) bombs make up the load of a Bristol Blenheim IV twin-engine bomber, 1941. The Blenheim IV, with its characteristic long nose, entered service in March 1939.*

If it is possible to state that there was a typical Lancaster, it was one with a top speed of 462km/h (287mph) at 3500m (11,500ft), a service ceiling of 7472m (24,500ft) and a range of 2671km (1660 miles) with a full 6356kg (14,000lb) bomb-load. It had three turrets, the nose and dorsal having two and the tail four 7.92mm (0.303in) machine-guns. The bomb bay was large enough to accommodate a 3632kg (8000lb) bomb, but the aircraft was able to lift the 5448kg (12,000lb) Tallboy and 9988kg (22,000lb) Grand Slam bombs. Both were carried semi-externally, as was the other, equally famous, 'special weapon' with which the Lancaster is associated: the 'bouncing bomb' that was used in May 1943 to breach the Moehne and Eder dams.

The Lancaster was used operationally for the first time on 3 March 1942, and after making its first 'hundred-bomber raid' on 31 July, it slowly established itself as the mainstay of Bomber Command. In the course of the war it flew 156,000 sorties and dropped 608,612 tonnes of bombs, suffering in the process a lower rate of attrition than any other British bomber. Ending the war dropping food to the starving Dutch, the Lancaster's wartime record has been inevitably dominated by three actions: the dams raid, the sinking of the battleship *Tirpitz* in November 1944, and the destruction of the Bielefeld viaduct in March 1945. Its wartime service with Coastal Command was slight but important, and after the war the Lancaster served as a maritime reconnaissance aircraft well after it had been withdrawn from service as a bomber. The last Lancaster was withdrawn from service with the RAF in 1956.

LEFT: *A Short Stirling four-engine heavy bomber dwarfs its crew, 1941. The Stirling, unlike both the Halifax and Lancaster, was designed from the start as a four-engine machine, and was the first of the trio to enter front-line squadron service with Bomber Command. Despite a prototype crash on 14 May 1939, the Stirling entered production in 1940 and No 7 Squadron flew the first operation using the new aircraft on 10/11 February 1941. The huge size of the Stirling may be seen from the photograph – the large undercarriage was necessary because of the wing incidence – and throughout its operational career the aircraft suffered from an inability to fly much higher than 4675m (15,000ft). At this altitude it was prey to German flak and night-fighters.*

BELOW: *Another view of the Stirling bomber, showing its relatively short wingspan – 30.5m (100ft) – imposed by an Air Ministry ruling in 1937 that the aircraft should be able to fit inside existing hangars. The Stirling was withdrawn from the bombing campaign by 1944, after which it was relegated largely to transport and glider-towing duties.*

The Night Fighter
The Messerschmitt
Bf-110F-4/G-4

Just as the Republic P-47 Thunderbolt proved a formidable aircraft in a role for which it was not intended, so the Messerschmitt Bf-110, after a devastatingly successful introduction to battle, found a role for itself as far removed from the original intention of its designers as it was possible to be. Pressed into service as a night-fighter, the Bf-110F-4 and Bf-110G-4 fought and won the Battle of Berlin between November 1943 and March 1944, although in the end their attempts to check and defeat the mounting Allied bombing offensive against the Reich proved in vain.

The Bf-110 began life on the drawing board in 1934 as a 'strategic fighter.' In common with other air forces of the day, the still-secret Luftwaffe thought in terms of deep-penetration operations by bombers, the Bf-110 being conceived as a *kampfzerstörer* (destroyer) that would hack enemy fighters from the skies and thereby clear a path for the bombers to their target. The endurance needed for such an aircraft could only be achieved on two engines, the Luftwaffe accepting the resultant loss of maneuverability on the part of a two-engine fighter on the basis of its superior firepower equalizing accounts in a dogfight with a single-engine fighter.

From the outset, the potential of the Bf-110 for multirole development was recognized by the Luftwaffe, as were the attendant dangers. The *zerstörer's* combination of long range, good speed and respectable armament and armor seemed to offer the prospect of a fighter, escort, interceptor, light bomber and close-support aircraft within a single product, the reverse side of the coin being that the Bf-110 might prove unable to discharge any role effectively. This prospect was discounted by Hermann Goering, but even the head of the Luftwaffe could not discount the problems presented by the lack of a suitable engine for the aircraft. As a result of delays, the Bf-110 emerged too late to see service in the Spanish Civil War (1936-39), but, available in numbers in the 'C' mark, it made an impressive entry to battle over Poland in 1939.

The Bf-110C confirmed its reputation in the course of the German offensive in the West in the spring of 1940, but in the Battle of Britain its inferiority and vulnerability to single-engine fighters was so marked that the Luftwaffe was forced to provide it with a Bf-109 escort. As a result of its poor showing, the Bf-110C was switched to less-demanding duties, but with subsequent modifications and additions and no corresponding increase in power, the performance of the Bf-110 declined, to the point where the decision to end production was inevitable. The assembly lines came to a halt between October and December 1941, but with the disastrous failure of the Me-210 program, they were reactivated in February 1942 with the result that the Bf-110E and Bf-110F, both heavy fighter-bombers, began to enter service in the spring and summer respectively.

Of the two, the Bf-110F proved the more significant because, with the new 1350hp engine, it was better suited to development than the Bf-110E, which remained underpowered by a 1100hp engine. Nevertheless, it was a Bf-110E that was first tested as a night-fighter, and it was one of the most unusual features of this particular aircraft, the Bf-110E-1/U-1, that was widely incorporated in subsequent Bf-110F-4 and Bf-110G-4 fighters and used to telling effect against British bombers. This was the *schrage musik* ('jazz music'), twin 20mm (0.8in) cannon firing forward and upward at an angle of 15 degrees from the vertical. Fired by the pilot with the aid

of a reflector sight, this allowed a night-fighter to attack a bomber from positions uncovered by the victim's guns.

Schrage musik accounted for many British bombers, most being raked by fire without ever seeing their attacker before, during or after the attack that resulted in their destruction. But this armament apart, the Bf-110F and even more powerfully engined Bf-110G proved well suited to night operations because at night their middling performance as aircraft was not important: they

RIGHT: *A German radar and anti-aircraft installation on the French coast in 1943-4. The radar shown is the* Würzburg *medium-range precision location type. These were used in conjunction with the longer-range* Freya *radars in the German defense system.*

BELOW: *A Bf-110G-4 of* Nachtjagdgeschwader *(Night-Fighter Group) 6, interned in Switzerland in 1944, displays its* FuG 202 Lichtenstein *air-interception radar aerial array. The two nose-mounted 30mm MK 108 cannon may be seen.*

ABOVE: *Luftwaffe personnel make final adjustments to the camera belonging to the photo-reconnaissance version of the Messerschmitt Bf-110D in the background. The evolution of the 'D' variant, with its long-range capability, made it an ideal PR machine, especially over the vast distances of North Africa.*

RIGHT: *A Messerschmitt Bf-110C of Zerstörergeschwader 52 flies over the White Cliffs of southern England during the early stages of the Battle of Britain, August 1940. Lack of maneuverability and speed meant the Zerstörers were condemned to destruction at the hands of the RAF.*

LEFT: *The covers come off a Heinkel He-111H of* Kampfgeschwader *(Bomber Group) 26, prior to a raid on England, 1940. The He-111H, developed in 1939, was powered by two Junkers Jumo 211 D-2 engines and could carry up to 2000kg (4400lb) of bombs over a range of 1207km (750 miles), but it was dangerously vulnerable to interception, as losses over England showed. It needed the close protection which the Messerschmitt Bf-110 proved unable to provide. In response, Heinkel designers added extra machine-guns – the 'H' had weapons in the nose, beam, ventral, dorsal and rear positions – but to little avail. By 1942 the He-111 was a vulnerable, obsolete aircraft.*

were stable gun platforms and could carry a heavy armament, and they had the space needed to accommodate the variety of radars, search receivers and radios that were essential if the aircraft was to function effectively in this role. Such was the pace of technological development after 1942 that the electronic equipment carried by Bf-110 night-fighters changed with almost bewildering rapidity, but the most significant advances that were registered had the effect of transforming the Bf-110f-4/G-4 from a fighter that could operate at night into a genuine night-fighter.

At the beginning of 1943 the Luftwaffe relied upon the *Himmelbett* system of defense against night bombing. This was a complicated command and control system that relied upon *Freya* radar to provide long-range detection of the enemy and two *Würzburg* radars to deal with individual aircraft, one to track an enemy bomber and the other to track a defending fighter. The plot was tracked on a device known as the '*Seeberg* Table' in what was popularly known to the Germans as the 'battle opera house,' the Luftwaffe's equivalent of a combat information center, and this command headquarters coordinated the tracks and talked the fighter toward its prey. With the *Himmelbett* system stretched across southern Denmark, western Germany, the Low Countries and northwest France, the demand on aircraft, radars and skilled manpower was enormous, but it proved very effective until the

summer of 1943. From spring 1943 onward the RAF began the jamming of German radio communications, and in July it introduced 'Window' (Chaff) in order to jam the *Würzburg* radars. The sudden inability of the Luftwaffe to track an enemy and lead fighters to their victims forced the Germans to intensify their search for a satisfactory airborne radar that operated on frequencies different from those of the *Würzburg* sets and to introduce VHF radios in the place of the HF sets used until that time. The most celebrated development was the *matratze* (mattress) with its proliferation of

---

Messerschmitt Bf-110G-4c

Type: Twin-engine night and all-weather fighter.
Performance: Max speed 550km/h (342mph).
Service ceiling 11,000m (36,090ft).
Range 2100km (1305 miles).
Armament: Two 30mm (1.2in), two 20mm (0.8in) cannon; one 7.92mm (0.303in) machine-gun.

BELOW: *Messerschmitt Bf-109F fighters provide close escort to a Junkers Ju-88 twin-engine bomber, 1942. Like the He-111, the Ju-88 was vulnerable to interception, hence the escort.*

aerials and antennas from the nose of the Bf-110, but these were gradually thinned as German radars improved down to ranges of 183m (600ft). Among the other electronics carried by Bf-110 night-fighters were a FuG 25 IFF set, a FuBl 2F navigation aid and the wingtip-mounted FuG 227/1 search receiver.

Supplied to Germany's three royal allies – Italy, Hungary and Romania – the Bf-110 night-fighters proved remarkably effective. They, plus flak and accidents, probably reached their maximum effectiveness on the night of 30/31 March 1944 when the British lost 96 bombers in the course of a single raid on Nuremberg, roughly 10 percent of the total force sent against the city. It was this operation that effectively ended the Battle of Berlin, Bomber Command being forced to admit that losses had become too great to be sustained. The switch of the bombing effort to France in support of the

forthcoming invasion left the Bf-110s in control of the night skies over Germany, but their victory was short-lived. By the last quarter of 1944 the Germans had lost control of the night sky, in part because the loss of the *Freya* posts denied the Germans the time they needed to concentrate their fighters against the incoming bomber stream, while the lack of sufficient numbers of Bf-110s coming off the production lines – plus an associated shortage of highly skilled pilots, training time and fuel – ensured that in meeting 'round-the-clock' bombing the night-fighters were worn down.

ABOVE: *A Dornier Do-215 twin-engine bomber, photographed over England, 1941. The Do-215 had a top speed of 400km/h (255mph).*
BELOW: *A Focke Wulf Fw-200 Condor – the only four-engine design to see widespread Luftwaffe service, but as a maritime patrol aircraft rather than a strategic bomber.*

LEFT: *Although the German raids on Britain in 1940-41 failed to achieve their aims of industrial disruption and civilian demoralization on a war-winning scale, they did disrupt the lives of ordinary people, particularly in London. One of the more obvious results was a need to shelter from the raids, and although the usual image is of civilians using the underground railway system, the government did provide purposebuilt communal shelters. This photograph shows one of these, for the people of the East End of London.*

BELOW: *A Dornier Do-217E in flight, 1940. A further development of the Do-17 Series, the 217 first appeared in August 1938 as a 'heavy' bomber, but its twin engines soon denied it that role. Used increasingly for other duties – notably reconnaissance and maritime strike – the 217 failed to live up to expectations. A 'K' variant of 1942 introduced a radically redesigned nose section, fully glazed and rounded.*

The Day Bomber
The Consolidated B-24
Liberator

Built in more variants and for more purposes than any other aircraft of World War II, the Consolidated B-24 Liberator was also built in greater numbers than any other aircraft in American history. Of the 97,810 bombers accepted into service between 1 July 1940 and 31 August 1945, no fewer than 18,188 were Liberators, total B-24 production being 19,203.

The Liberator's production record is somewhat surprising given the fact it was both a more complicated and expensive aircraft than Boeing's B-17 Flying Fortress yet in overall performance was not appreciably superior to its much older colleague. The sheer volume of B-24 production reduced labor-requirements per unit by 41 percent between January 1943 and January 1944 and overall unit costs by 43 percent between 1941 and 1944, but at war's end the Liberator remained the most expensive combat aircraft in the American inventory with the obvious exception of the B-29 Superfortress. Moreover, it was an aircraft with three main builders – Consolidated, Douglas and Ford – and more than 100 major subcontractors, and such was the industrial effort and investment involved in Liberator production that the main center, Willow Run, in 1944 produced under a single roof airframe equivalent to half that produced by the entire German aviation industry.

Requested by the US Army Air Corps (AAC) in 1939 as a bomber with a 4827km (3000 mile) range and a top speed of more than 483km/h (300 mph), the prototype Liberator first flew on 29 December 1939, production orders having been previously received from the AAC, Britain and France. In British service even before delivery to the recently renamed US Army Air Force (AAF) began in March 1941, the Liberator quickly progressed to the 'C' variant, the first major production version, and the B-24D, which had turbocharged engines, and more fuel and armor, a better defensive armament and heavier bomb-load than earlier Liberator versions. It was this latter mark of B-24, serving with RAF Coastal

ABOVE: _B-24s of the 458th Bomb Group, Eighth USAAF, fly in formation toward their target in Germany, 1944. Incoming fighters had to face a formidable defensive fire._
FAR LEFT: _Consolidated B-24J Liberators of the Eighth USAAF Bomb Tours, 15 June 1944, as part of the interdiction campaign in support of the Normandy landings._

Command as the Liberator III, IIIA or V, that proved of critical importance in ensuring Allied victory in the Battle of the Atlantic in the spring of 1943.

The Liberator's role in closing the 'air gap' south of Greenland and Iceland was the direct result of its having an operational range greater than that of any other land-based aircraft, and it was this asset that in 1942 prompted the American decision to use in future only the B-24 in the Pacific. In the European theater of operations, however, the B-24 was the junior of the heavy bombers, the US Eighth Army Air Force being adamant in its preference for the Flying Fortress. In May 1945 only 11 groups of the Eighth were equipped solely with Liberators in contrast to the 20 equipped only with B-17s. In the Mediterranean theater of operations, on the other hand, the Liberator outnumbered the B-17 by three-to-one, its ability to attack targets deep in the Balkans from bases in North Africa and southern Italy being an important factor in its predominance in this command. The relative disfavor with which the Liberator was viewed by the Eighth Army Air Force was the result of the fact that whereas the early variants had been weak in terms of armor and guns, improvements worked into later versions made for instability. The Liberator had a certain reputation for not being an easy aircraft to fly.

Nevertheless, in its most numerous form, the 6678-strong 'J' variant, the Liberator was a formidable aircraft. Capable of a maximum speed of 467km/h (290mph) at 8021m (26,500ft) and with a service ceiling of 9150m (30,000ft), the B-24J had 3540km (2200 mile) range

FAR LEFT: *B-24s of the Fifteenth USAAF hit Ploesti, 15 May 1944.*
LEFT: *Flight and ground crew of an Eighth AAF B-17.*
BELOW: *B-24 'Diamond Lil': a surviving, unarmed example.*

with a 2270kg (5000lb) bomb-load. Its normal maximum bomb-load was 3995kg (8800lb), but it had provision to carry a further 1816kg (4000lb) of bombs externally on short-haul missions. Defensively it was armed with four twin turrets and two single waist positions, all with 12.7mm (0.5in) machine-guns, and with these and their bombs, Liberators claimed to have accounted for more than 4000 enemy aircraft in the course of the war. In action with American forces in November 1941, the Liberator saw service as a bomber, transport, tanker, reconnaissance, patrol and antisubmarine aircraft, and saw employment with the US Navy and various British Commonwealth air forces in addition to the AAF. In various noncombat roles the Liberator continued to see service into the early 1960s.

Consolidated B-24J Liberator
Type: Four-engine heavy bomber.
Performance: Max speed 467km/h (290mph).
Service ceiling 9150m (30,000ft).
Range 3540km (2200 miles).
Armament: 10 12.7mm (0.5in) machine-guns; 5811kg (12,800lb) max bomb-load.

The Role of the Medium Bomber
The North American B-25 Mitchell

The most widely used American bomber of World War II, the North American B-25 Mitchell was employed on bombing, attack, antisubmarine, antishipping and general reconnaissance duties in the southwest Pacific, China, southeast Asia, the North Atlantic, North Africa and throughout the Mediterranean theater of operations, and in northwest Europe. In its many roles it saw service not only with the United States Army Air Force (USAAF), for which it was built, but with the British, Dutch and Soviet air forces and with

the US Navy. It is best remembered as the bomber used in the Doolittle Raid on Tokyo on 18 April 1942, though less well known is the fact that the B-25 was the first bomber to hit Japan from a land base, Paramushiru being struck by Mitchells of the US Eleventh Air Force operating from Attu Island on 10 July 1943.

Ordered in 1939 straight from the drawing board of a company with no previous experience of designing either twin-engine bombers or military aircraft of any kind, and without a factory to

RIGHT: *A North American B-25 Mitchell medium bomber of the 488th Bomb Squadron, 340th Bomb Group, Twelfth USAAF, flies over the devastated Benedictine monastery at Cassino, 15 February 1944. This particular raid was one of the most controversial of the war, involving the destruction of one of the most historic buildings in Italy, but it was deemed necessary because of tough German defenses in the Cassino area. The attack coincided with a ground assault on Monastery Hill by the 4th Indian Division, but the Germans, having survived the bombing, managed to put up a solid defense. It was to take another three months of fighting to seize Cassino.*

LEFT: *Surviving B-25 Mitchell bombers are gathered at Blackbushe airfield in Hampshire for a filming session. The front aircraft – 'Big Bad Bonnie' – is a B-25J, characterized by the turret just aft of the cockpit. Existing in both solid and glazed nose variants, the 'J' was probably the best medium bomber of World War II: formidably armed with up to 18 machine-guns and capable of carrying up to 1816kg (4000lb) of bombs, it saw action in every theater. More examples of the B-25 seem to have survived in flying condition than any other aircraft type from the war years.*

mass produce its intended wares, the B-25 first flew in August 1940, entering service in February 1941. From the outset of its career, however, it was subjected to in-service modification and development characteristic of all good aircraft. The most important of the early changes were the introduction of a gull wing and horizontal wing sections outboard of the engine nacelles in the place of unbroken dihedrals; the installation of armor and self-sealing tanks; and, with the B-25B, the suppression of the rear-gun position along with the incorporation of a power-driven dorsal turret and a retractable ventral turret. The various changes resulted in a medium bomber that in its first mass-produced form – as the B-25C built at Inglewood in California and the B-25D built at Kansas City –

North American B-25D Mitchell
Type: Twin-engine medium bomber.
Performance: Max speed 507km/h (315mph).
Service ceiling 8235m (23,500ft).
Range 2172km (1350 miles).
Armament: Four 12.7mm (0.5in) and one 7.62mm (0.3in) machine-guns; up to 1362kg (3000lb) bomb-load.

---

had two 1700hp radial engines and a top speed of 507km/h (315mph), a service ceiling of 8235m (23,500ft) and a range of 2172km (1350 miles) with a 1362kg (3000lb) payload. It was with the first three marks of B-25 that the United States entered the war in December 1941, when it was being operationally employed on antisubmarine patrols in both the Pacific and the North Atlantic.

Despite its many good qualities, combat quickly revealed that the Mitchell was poorly armed defensively and inadequately equipped to operate in the low-level attack role. The answer to both problems in part lay in strengthening the forward-firing

armament, a procedure that was improvised in operational theaters with regard to existing aircraft and then built into certain production variants, the B-25J, for example, being built with a version that had a solid nose cone and eight fixed 12.7mm (0.5in) cannon. The J edition of the Mitchell was also noted for being the first mark with the dorsal turret moved forward to a position just aft of the cockpit, and in common with other marks the B-25J also had provision for fuselage-mounted twin cannon. More impressively, the B-25G (a direct modification of the B-25C) and B-25H were built with variants equipped with a forward-firing 75mm (3in) artillery

ABOVE: *An extremely dramatic photograph, showing a Japanese frigate under air attack from B-25 Mitchell medium bombers of the 345th Bomb Group, Solomons area, 1943. Taken from the rear gun position of a Mitchell which has just made its bombing run, the photograph shows another B-25 in the process of dropping its bombs, while a third aircraft comes in behind. The ship is moving at speed in an effort to escape and is putting up defensive fire from two 4in guns and a host of machine-guns. Attacks such as this were an essential part of the air war in the Pacific.*

LEFT: *One of the specially converted B-25B Mitchells takes off for Tokyo from the deck of the carrier USS Hornet, 18 April 1942. Led by Lieutenant-Colonel James Doolittle, 16 B-25s set off to bomb the Japanese capital, flying on from there to friendly territory in China. In psychological terms, the raid was a success, boosting the morale of the Allies while undermining that of the Japanese, who believed their homeland to be beyond the range of US aircraft, but the cost was high (few of the raiders survived) and the actual damage to Tokyo was slight.*

LEFT: *A Martin B-26 Marauder medium bomber in its death throes over Toulon, 1944. The aircraft has just been hit by 88mm antiaircraft fire, which has completely severed the starboard engine from its mounting, causing the wheel hydraulics to fail and the main landing wheel to flop down. In such circumstances, there was little the pilot could do to save his ship: within seconds, it had plunged to destruction in the center of Toulon. The B-26, a compact and streamlined twin-engine design, first flew in November 1940 and, despite some problems in the early months of production, went on to serve effectively in all theaters of war. Its Pratt and Whitney Double Wasp radial engines gave it a top speed of 490km/h (305mph), and it could carry a bomb-load of 1362kg (3000lb).*

BELOW: *Eight of the B-25Bs used on the Doolittle raid on Tokyo, 18 April 1942, stand exposed to the elements on the deck of USS Hornet as Task Force 16 moves to a position within range of the Japanese homeland. Because of the size of the B-25s and their lack of folding wings, they could not be placed inside the Hornet's hangars and had to travel on deck. This left little room for take-off, increasing the already tremendous risks of the operation. When Lieutenant-Colonel Doolittle led his force off the carrier at 0820 hours on 18 April, no one could be absolutely sure of success.*

TOP: *A Lockheed 414 Hudson medium bomber. Developed hurriedly from the Lockheed Model 14 airliner in response to a request from the British in 1938, the Hudson proved more suited to maritime than land operations.*
ABOVE: *Douglas Boston medium bombers of the RAF. The Boston was based on the Douglas DB-7 design and over 1200 served with the RAF from 1940 until the end of World War II.*
LEFT: *A Martin B-26 Marauder in flight, 1944. Nicknamed 'Dee Feater,' the aircraft has already carried out 48 missions.*

piece, the largest gun (firing a 9kg/20lb shell) ever carried operationally by an aircraft. In a low-level attack role the firepower that Mitchells with such an armament could put down on an enemy, particularly enemy shipping, was formidable.

The B-25J, which accounted for 4318 of the total of 9816 Mitchells built, was also noted for improved armor protection. Individual crew members were given enhanced protection, while longitudinal armor was worked into the aircraft in order to prevent strafing through the length of the Mitchell. In addition, the last 1600 B-25Js were fitted with armored deflectors and fairings for their upper turret.

The various changes worked into the later Mitchells inevitably reduced speed, which fell to a maximum of 410km/h (255mph) at 4575m (15,000ft). A combat range of over 2092km (1300 miles) and existing bomb-load, however, were maintained. Indeed, with external racks which were introduced with the B-25C, the carrying capacity of the later Mitchells was set at 1816kg (4000lb), more than that of the original B-25A and B-25B, and the B-25J was able to carry a torpedo or six depth-charges as alternatives to bombs. In overall terms, the result was an aircraft that was not without its critics, who generally preferred the Marauder or Mosquito for certain types of operations, but which nevertheless was probably the best medium bomber of World War II.

The Bombing of Japan
The Boeing B-29 Superfortress

The desire on the part of the United States to be the owner of a bomber with a range of 8045km (5000 miles), a speed in excess of 322km/h (200mph) and a 908kg (2000lb) payload dates back to 1933. The technology of the day, however, did not allow the required engine-power-to-aircraft-size ratio to be realized, but the work that went into developing the ill-fated Boeing B-15 and Douglas B-19 projects proved of value in the eventual fulfillment of somewhat less ambitious programs.

Official interest in the project survived the disappointments of the 1930s, however, and in January 1940 the government issued a specification requirement for a very long-range heavy bomber to four companies. Preliminary contracts were issued in the following June, but with the early withdrawal of Lockheed and Douglas from proceedings Boeing, with the B-29 project, and Consolidated, with its B-32 rival, were left to develop and construct the only very

heavy bombers built by any nation in World War II. In the event, however, the B-32 program was maintained only as insurance against the B-29 program failing. A total of 118 B-32s were built before the end of the war, and of these only 15 were to see service in the Pacific.

Such was the confidence of the Army Air Force (AAF) in the B-29 venture, on the other hand, that it placed a production order for 1664 Superfortresses before the first prototype was flown in September 1942. Such confidence was nevertheless an act of faith, and the project was often referred to as 'the three-billion dollar gamble' for the risks it ran, on four main counts. First, even before the aircraft was delivered into service, American strategic policy for the war against Japan was altered in order to secure island bases from which it could operate against Japan, it being assumed that the final product would meet design requirements. Second,

with factories fully committed to existing orders, four massive new factories had to be built and equipped from nothing in order to build the B-29. Third, the demand of the B-29 on scarce resources was all but prohibitive, the airframe alone requiring the materials needed to build 11 Mustangs and the overall requirements of the B-29 being equivalent to those of three B-17s or B-24s. Fourth, in order to get the B-29 into service quickly, the AAF had to dispense with the test and evaluation program that its advanced qualities demanded. Nevertheless, the gamble paid off with 3763 Super-fortresses delivered to the AAF by the end of the war, at which time 2132 were in service with 21 fully operational squadrons.

ABOVE: *'Little Boy,' the atomic bomb dropped from B-29 Enola Gay onto Hiroshima, 6 August 1945. The bomb contained two pieces of Uranium 235, blasted together to create an explosion.*
ABOVE LEFT: *The distinctive mushroom cloud of an atomic explosion marks the destruction of Nagasaki in Japan, 9 August 1945. The bomb was dropped by B-29 Superfortress Bock's Car.*
BELOW: *Boeing B-29 Superfortress Enola Gay of the 509th Composite Group. Piloted by Colonel Paul Tibbetts, this aircraft dropped the atomic bomb on Hiroshima.*

ABOVE: *A Boeing B-29 Superfortress VLR (Very Long Range) bomber shows its sleek lines during a test-flight prior to squadron delivery, 1944. First flown on 21 September 1942, the B-29 was a sophisticated design.*

TOP RIGHT: *A B-29 shows its various gun positions to advantage: a 20mm cannon and twin 0.5in machine-guns in the tail, with two 0.5in machine-guns in each of four remote-controlled turrets.*

LEFT: *The aftermath of the atomic strike against Nagasaki: when the bomb was dropped on the city early on 9 August 1945, 39,000 people died instantly.*

RIGHT: *B-29s of the 468th Bomb Group, 58th Bombardment Wing, drop their bombs over Rangoon, Burma, 1944. Deployed initially to China, the B-29s found it difficult to hit Japan, despite their effective range of 4486km (2850 miles): it was not until the Mariana Islands became available as a base that the campaign began to bite.*

In technical terms the B-29 was all the AAF could have asked. With four 2200hp engines, each with two exhaust-driven turbo-superchargers, the B-29 could attain a maximum speed of 604km/h (375mph) at 9714m (31,850ft) and had a combat range of 6597km (4100 miles) with a 4540kg (10,000lb) bomb-load. Its maximum bomb-load was 9080kg (20,000lb) under normal circumstances but it was able to carry two 9988kg (22,000lb) 'Grand Slam' bombs and, of course, it was able to carry atomic weapons. Defensively, the Superfortress was equipped with a central fire control system, four fuselage turrets each with two machine-guns and a rear turret position. With a service ceiling of 9714m (31,850ft), the B-29 was fully pressurized. In terms of effectiveness, however, the first B-29 operations left much to be desired.

Denied a role in Europe, the B-29 initially saw service in Southeast Asia and China, its first operations being from bases in India against Bangkok on 5 June 1944 and from Chinese airfields against Yawata, on Kyushu, 10 days later. The first B-29 operation against Japan from the Marianas took place on 24 November, but in all operations before the end of February 1945 B-29 attacks suffered from two problems. First, relatively few Superfortresses were available for operations, and for success the B-29 was no different from other bombers in that it needed to attack in large numbers, which were not available at the time. Second, initial attacks were made at high altitude and here the Superfortresses encountered winds that dispersed bomb-loads and played havoc with engines. As a result, in March 1945 the B-29s were order to carry out low-level incendiary attacks at night against Japanese cities. The outcome was frightfully impressive. Between 9 March and 14 August B-29s, usually numbering between 450 and 550 on any single raid, laid waste not merely 'the big five' – Tokyo, Nagoya, Osaka, Kobe and Kawasaki-Yokohama – but 51 of the 58 secondary cities attacked in that period. At the same time, the B-29s carried out the greatest aerial mining campaign in history and regularly flew tactical air strikes in support of naval forces off Okinawa. Their efforts, of course, came to an awful climax at Hiroshima and Nagasaki in August 1945, and herein lies the Superfortress' enduring claim to fame – and one that hopefully will never be challenged: it was the only aircraft to use atomic weapons operationally. War would never be the same again.

Boeing B-29 Superfortress
Type: Four-engine very long-range heavy bomber.
Performance: Max speed 604km/h (375mph).
Service ceiling 9714m (31,850ft).
Range 6597km (4100 miles).
Armament: One 20mm (0.8in) cannon; 10 12.7mm (0.5in) machine-guns; 9080kg (20,000lb) maximum bomb-load.

NAVAL AVIATION

ABOVE: *A Mitsubishi A6M5 Navy Type O Carrier Fighter Model 52 – Zero fighter – in flight, 1945. As a carrier-borne fighter, the Zero was in a class of its own by 1941, combining speed, rate of climb and maneuverability to match any land-based equivalent. It was not until the Japanese naval air service had been weakened by heavy pilot losses in battles such as Midway (June 1942) and Guadalcanal (August 1942 to February 1943) that the Allies were able to counter the myth of Zero invincibility, and not until the appearance of US fighters such as the Hellcat and Corsair that air superiority was regained.*

RIGHT: *A Japanese pilot fixes his patriotic headband before embarking on a kamikaze suicide mission, 1945. The idea of using aircraft to crash into American surface ships was first introduced on 15 October 1944, when a Yokosuka D4Y dive-bomber peeled off from a 90-plane formation massed above US Task Force 38.4 and deliberately flew into the aircraft carrier USS Franklin, starting fires and killing many of the crew. Flown by Rear Admiral Arima, this* kamikaze *(literally, 'Divine Wind') mission was emulated by hundreds of Japanese pilots in the last months of the war.*

The Carrier Fighter
The Mitsubishi A6M Zero

In common with the US Navy in the interwar period, the Imperial Japanese Navy (IJN) settled upon a tactical doctrine that stressed offensive action on the part of its carriers. Both navies built and trained their carriers to seek out and destroy their opposite numbers, the Japanese placing their trust in dive-bombers to find enemy carriers and account for their flight decks.

As part of this doctrine the IJN envisaged its fighters sweeping aside their enemy counterparts and thus allowing the dive-bombers to attack under the most favorable of conditions. In a wider context, the IJN envisaged operating fleet and amphibious forces behind a front secured by its fighters. In order to secure air supremacy, therefore, the IJN sought to acquire two things: a corps of highly trained, long-service airmen, plus fighters of exceptional quality. In both efforts its was successful, the A6M Zero being one of the very few naval fighters of World War II able to match contemporary land-based fighters.

The A6M began life in May 1937 when the IJN laid down specifications for a replacement for the A5M Claude, which had yet to enter service. Subsequently these requirements were tightened, the product ultimately demanded being a fighter with a top speed of 500km/h (310mph) at 3965m (13,000ft), the ability to climb to 3050m (10,000ft) in 3.5 mintues, a range of two hours at cruising speed or eight hours at an economical cruising speed of 322km/h (200mph). In addition, the fighter was to carry two 20mm (0.8in) cannon and two 7.7mm (0.3in) machine-guns, have provision for a 113kg (250lb) bomb-load, and be fitted with radio and direction-finding equipment. As if such demands did not pose problems enough, the final requirement was for an aircraft that could take off in less than 67m (220ft). Such demands were so severe that one major company, Nakajima, refused to consider the project.

Mitsubishi, however, tendered, completed its designs in April 1938 and built its first prototype in March 1939. By using a small but powerful radial engine of 875hp and an exceptionally small framework that incorporated every possible weight-saving device, Mitsubishi produced an aircraft that met or exceeded every design requirement. By using lightweight Extra Super-Duralumin extensively in the airframe, fabric in the wings and by dispensing with strengtheners deemed essential in Western aircraft, Mitsubishi

BELOW: *A Japanese* kamikaze *pilot flies perilously close to the deck of the American battleship USS* Missouri, *28 April 1945. In the event, the aircraft was shot down before hitting the ship.*

produced an aircraft that swept all before it in the Pacific and Southeast Asia after December 1941.

The tragedy of the Zero, and indeed the tragedy for the Japanese in their entire war effort, was that initial success could not be consolidated – which in the case of the Zero meant that the aircraft was incapable of substantial qualitative improvement. In effect a one-shot weapon, the Zero was formidable in its intended attack role in 1941 and 1942, particularly in the hands of an experienced pilot, but with an airframe that weighed less than 1816kg (4000lb) the A6M was not able to absorb the changes needed to enable it to fight defensively. Its lack of armor and self-sealing tanks, sacrificed in order to boost range and agility, left the Zero vulnerable to the heavy firepower of American fighters, while the peculiar construction requirements of the aircraft – in particular the need to build the wing spar as part of the fuselage and the wings as complete units – did not lend themselves easily to simple mass-production techniques. Despite being built in greater number (10,449) than any other Japanese fighter and being subjected to development in terms of greater engine, armor and self-sealing tanks, the Zero was outnumbered by any one of the four main fighters in American service in the Pacific War. Moreover, each of these fighters, the Thunderbolt, Mustang, Hellcat and Corsair, could match the performance of the Zero in every respect with the exception of range, and, of course, by the end of the war quality pilots were almost the sole preserve of the United States. The Zero remained in service until August 1945 in a number of roles and variants, although after 1942 it became less effective in a war which it had begun but in which the Americans rewrote the script.

Mitsubishi A6M3 Zero
Type: Single-engine carrier-borne fighter.
Performance: Max speed 544km/h (338mph).
Service ceiling 11,050m (36,250ft).
Range 2377km (1477 miles).
Armament: Two 20mm (0.8in) cannon, two 7.7mm (0.3in) machine-guns.

TOP LEFT: *A Mitsubishi A6M Zero fighter, given the tail markings of the* Oitu Kokutai *(Naval Air Corps), 1944.*

BELOW LEFT: *The American carrier USS* Hornet *comes under air attack from an Aichi D3A 'Val' dive-bomber and a Nakajima B5N 'Kate' torpedo-bomber, Solomons, 1942.*

RIGHT: *A Yokosuka MXY7 Ohka ('Cherry Blossom') rocket-propelled suicide aircraft, captured on Okinawa, 1945.*

BELOW: *A surviving example of a Nakajima B5N2 'Kate' torpedo-bomber of the type used at Pearl Harbor, December 1941.*

Carrier Strike
The Grumman TBF Avenger

ABOVE: *A TBF-1 Avenger launches its torpedo from its weapons bay. The ventral 0.3in machine-gun may be seen just below the fuselage marking.*

FAR LEFT: *Grumman TBF Avenger torpedo-bombers in formation over the Pacific, 1943. Avengers first saw action at the Battle of Midway on 4 June 1942.*

LEFT: *The might of the US Pacific Fleet: Task Group 38.3 enters Ulithi anchorage December 1944. In the lead, with TBF Avengers on deck, is the carrier USS* Langley, *with USS* Ticonderoga *and the battleship* Washington *behind.*

In service with the US Navy for 15 years without any major structural modification, the TBF Avenger was ordered in 1940 from Grumman as a replacement for the obsolescent Douglas TBD Devastator. First flown in August 1941, the Grumman product entered service in January 1942 as an all-metal monoplane (albeit with fabric-covered control surfaces), with a midwing configuration and the distinctively chunky, Grumman profile. With rear-folding wings for ease of handling and storage in a carrier's hangar, the TBF-1 had a 1700hp engine, a top speed of 414km/h (257mph) at 3660m (12,000ft), a range of 1778km (1105 miles) with a 559mm (22in) torpedo or 908kg (2000lb) bomb-load, and good low-speed handling characteristics. It accommodated a three-man crew and was defensively armed with three machine-guns, though certain later variants carried additional guns in the wings.

The TBF Avenger entered service when the demand for torpedo-bombers was intense. In March 1942, therefore, General Motors' Eastern Division, which was then building F4F Wildcat fighters, was contracted to produce Avengers. With production

beginning in September that year and the first aircraft delivered into service two months later, General Motors' finished article was designated the TBM. Subsequent development of the Avenger by Grumman and General Motors was in tandem, but production was not: of the 9839 Avengers built, General Motors accounted for 7546. It was the scale of Avenger production, by far the largest of any carrier aircraft with the exceptions of the Corsair and Hellcat, that enabled the United States to supply 921 to the Royal Navy and 63 to the Royal New Zealand Air Force and to diversify into specific variants for a number of roles.

The Avenger's prime role was as a torpedo-bomber, but its combination of good payload and long range meant that it was well suited to other duties. In Royal Navy service it was used for antisubmarine work from escort carriers, though its being used in this role was in part the result of its incompatibility with British torpedoes. The British carriers that entered the Pacific in 1945, however, had no other strike aircraft but the Avenger, which was employed as a level-altitude bomber and, incongruously, as a dive-bomber. In

RIGHT: *Grumman TBF Avenger torpedo-bombers, wings folded and engines warming up, are readied for take-off from the deck of the carrier USS* Enterprise, *May 1944. In the foreground, another Avenger is being brought up on deck from the hangar below. The* Enterprise, *laid down in 1936, took part in more engagements than any other US warship in World War II, earning 19 battle stars. She was scrapped in 1958.*

BOTTOM RIGHT: *An F-4U Corsair pictured at an air show in 1986. The Corsair was perhaps the most effective naval fighter produced during World War II. It was the first US Navy aircraft capable of exceeding 400mph in level flight. The Corsair fought in all the major battles of the Pacific War from 1943 on and was still in service during the Korean War.*

BELOW: *A TBF Avenger comes in to land on the deck of an American 'Essex'-class carrier, Pacific Theater, 1944. The Americans designed their carriers to provide a clear flight-deck, uncluttered with defensive gun positions, in order that a maximum number of aircraft could be launched or recovered at any one time.*

American service, specialist roles were forced upon the Avenger by the changing pattern of the Pacific War. Japanese recourse to night operations led to Avengers being fitted with a short-range radar and given the task to lead two escorting fighters to an enemy intruder after themselves being led to an interception position by shipborne radar. This complicated arrangement was only a stop-gap measure designed to tide the fleet over until the time when radar-equipped night-fighters became available in strength. Radar, of the air-to-ship variety, also provided the Avenger with a scouting role, an important function in the last two years of the war, given the decline in the number of Dauntlesses and Hellcats with individual carriers. Enemy radar, moreover, provided yet another role, this time enabling the Avenger to operate as an electronic countermeasures (ECM) aircraft which was often backed by night-intruder operations. To add to the Avenger's effectiveness in the attack, a strengthening of wings allowed the housing of 89mm (3.5in) rockets, an improvement that was vital in terms of survival chances for a relatively slow aircraft, called upon to tackle heavily defended targets in Japan in the last months of the war. The Avenger was also scheduled for modification as an airborne early-warning aircraft, but the first squadron to be deployed for these duties arrived in the Pacific too late to see combat.

After the war the Avenger continued in front-line service with the US Navy until 1954. It was mainly involved in antisubmarine and ECM operations, but it continued to serve in other, lesser roles until 1957. It also saw two periods of employment with the Royal Navy, between 1945 and 1946 and between 1953 and 1955. It also served with the Royal Canadian Navy with Aeronavale and, ironically, with the Japanese Maritime Self-Defense Force.

Grumman TBF Avenger

Type: Single-engine torpedo-bomber.
Performance: Max speed 414km/h (257mph).
Service ceiling 6832m (22,400ft).
Range 1178km (1105 miles).
Armament: Three 12.7mm (0.5in) and one 7.62mm (0.3in) machine-guns; one 559mm (22in) torpedo; 908kg (2000lb) bomb-load.

The Flying Boat
The Kawanishi H6K Mavis and H8K Emily

Western histories of World War II and of military aviation have generally afforded full and proper treatment of such flying boats as the Consolidated PBY Catalina and the Short S.25 Sunderland: both the separate and combined contributions that these two flying boats made to the Allied victory in the Battle of the Atlantic have been properly documented and acknowledged. In contrast, all but unnoted by such histories are the flying boats like the Kawanishi H6K Mavis and H8K Emily, and this situation prevails despite the fact that the latter was qualitatively vastly superior to its opposite numbers in American and British service. Indeed, it had a performance superior to that of any flying boat produced by a Western nation for many years after 1945.

Both before and during World War II, the navies and air forces of all major powers built and used flying boats on general reconnaissance, antisubmarine, scouting, spotting, liaison and air-sea rescue duties. No navy, however, made as much use of these machines as the Imperial Japanese Navy (IJN), whose various products ranged from the tiny E14Y Glen seaplane, embarked in

submarines for scouting purposes, through the A6M2-N Rufe seaplane-fighter and a number of shipborne reconnaissance and spotting seaplanes, to the massively imposing Mavis and Emily. Such diversity, however, ultimately constituted weakness. Japan lacked the resources to sustain such proliferation, and the critical weakness of her flying boats – other than the collapse of the combat sections of naval aviation – was inadequacy of numbers. In contrast to the 4000 or so Catalinas built, the entire output of all types of H6K and H8K was just 215 and 167 respectively.

The Mavis set down as a design requirement in 1934, was Japan's first home-produced flying boat. It emerged in July 1936 as an exceedingly graceful high-wing, parasol monoplane with four 840hp radial engines. It entered production, however, with 1000hp engines, and in its final form as the H6K5, built when Kawanishi was developing the Emily, it carried 1300hp powerplants. In its standard H6K4 form, the Mavis was able to carry either two 800kg (1764lb), 533mm (21in) torpedoes or twelve 60kg (132lb) bombs on parallel struts, and with such payloads it had a range of 6771km

ABOVE: An H6K Mavis found in a hangar at Sourabaya in the Dutch East Indies (Indonesia) in 1945. Japanese markings may be seen beneath the wing, together with the green surrender crosses, but of equal interest are the Indonesian markings (on the wing) and the Dutch colors (on the fuselage).

FAR LEFT: A Kawanishi H6K Mavis flying boat goes down in flames after an encounter with an American fighter, May 1944. First flown in 1936, the H6K had a useful range of 6771km (4208 miles).

LEFT: A Blohm und Voss Bv-138C long-range reconnaissance flying boat – Der Fliegende Holzschuh ('Flying Clog'). First flown on 15 July 1937, the Bv-138 was beset with development problems, but the 'C' variant, produced in 1941, powered by three Junkers Jumo 205D engines, proved a useful flying boat.

151

LEFT: *A Short Sunderland long-range maritime reconnaissance flying boat. The Sunderland was a sound design, particularly in its Mark III configuration, which enjoyed a top speed of 338km/h (210mph), a range of over 4667km (2900 miles) and an endurance of more than 16 hours. The Mark III fairly bristled with guns, with eight 0.303in machine-guns in nose, dorsal and tail positions.*

BELOW: *Kawanishi H8K2 Emily long-range maritime reconnaissance flying-boat of the 801st Kokutai (Naval Air Corps), shortly after its capture by the Americans in 1945. The H8K2 model was armed with five 20mm Type 99 cannon in nose, dorsal and tail turrets and two beam hatches, and four 7.7mm machine-guns.*

FAR RIGHT, BELOW: *An American PBY-5A Catalina on patrol over the Aleutian Islands late in the war.*

(4208 miles). In a reconnaissance role the Mavis was able to stay airborne for more than 24 hours.

The Mavis, therefore, had excellent range, good speed – a maximum of 385km/h (239mph) with the H6K5 – and good payload to add to its impressive hydrodynamic qualities, but in common with other IJN aircraft of this period such attributes were secured at the expense of armor, self-sealing tanks and defensive armament. Combat was to reveal that it was an easy kill for the prowling fighters of a combat air patrol. The Emily, on the other hand, proved a much tougher proposition, though in its original form it represented no substantial improvement over the Mavis in terms of ability to absorb damage. Ordered in 1938, this high-wing flying boat was equipped with four 1530hp radial engines and was initially dogged by a succession of development problems, the most serious of which related to planing properties. A redesigned hull and nose cured the Emily's aversion to water, but it was only through the massive increase of power loading, made possible by the introduction of 1850hp engines, that the Emily emerged as a formidable long-range reconnaissance flying boat. Armor, the most elaborate protection of fuel tanks ever given to a Japanese aircraft, plus nine cannon and machine-guns, made the Emily more than a match for the Mavis, and it was able to equal the latter's range when used in the torpedo-attack and reconnaissance roles. Moreover, it was much faster than its predecessor, being able to make a

top speed of 467km/h (290mph) at 5000m (16,400ft) and a cruising speed of 296km/h (184mph) at 1220m (4000ft).

Though the Emily made its operational debut in March 1942 when two H8K1 boats, after staging through French Frigate Shoals from the Marshalls, bombed Oahu, it did not enter service in any appreciable numbers until the following year, by which time the tide of war had turned decisively against Japan. As a result, the Emily was forced to operate under increasingly unfavorable conditions, and despite valiant service and the provision of air-to-surface radar, its effectiveness declined in step with the IJN as a whole. Only a handful of Mavis and Emily flying boats remained to be surrendered in September 1945. Ultimately, of course, even the flying boats of the victorious Western powers were to travel the same, if less violent, path into history, the US Navy ending its flying-boat operations in 1961. At the present time just two major powers continue to operate military flying boats: the Soviet Union and, appropriately in view of the Mavis and Emily, Japan. Those in service with the latter's Maritime Self-Defense Force are worthy successors to machines that were, paradoxically, ahead of their time but inadequate for their own era.

Kawanishi H6K5 Mavis
Type: Four-engine long-range maritime reconnaissance flying boat.
Performance: Max speed 385km/h (239mph).
Service ceiling 9600m (31,365ft).
Range 6771km (4208 miles).
Armament: One 20mm (0.8in) cannon; four 7.7mm (0.3in) machine-guns; two 800kg (1764lb) torpedoes; 3000kg (6615lb) bomb-load.

Kawanishi H8K2 Emily
Type: Four-engine long-range maritime reconnaissance flying boat.
Performance: Max speed 467km/h (290mph).
Service ceiling 9120m (29,950ft).
Range 7176km (4460 miles).
Armament: Five 20mm (0.8in) cannon; four 7.7mm (0.3in) machine-guns; two 800kg (1764lb) torpedoes; 4500kg (9922lb) bomb-load.

The Seaplane
The Vought-Sikorsky OS2U Kingfisher

From the American perspective, the story of the Pacific War is one told primarily in terms of the fast carrier force. Where concessions are made to other services and branches of the Navy, Marine Corps and Army Air Force, land-based aviation is afforded the treatment of *primus inter pares*. The story, therefore, is one that is heavily dominated by the famous American aircraft of World War II, and amid the claims and counter-claims of the Corsair, Lightning and Hellcat, the Dauntless and Helldiver, the Mitchell and Marauder, the Liberator and Superfortress, it is too easy to lose sight of the fact that probably only one American aircraft served in the front-line throughout the Pacific War. That aircraft was the Vought-Sikorsky OS2U Kingfisher, which mounted search patrols from Pearl Harbor on 'the day of infamy' and was present in Tokyo Bay on 2 September 1945 when hostilities were brought to an end.

Before 1941 seaplanes formed a very important part of the fleet inventory of all the major powers. The OS designation applied by the Americans to their seaplanes with their battleships and cruisers was an acknowledgment of the dual role: when embarked in a battleship to observe and correct fire and when in a cruiser to act as scout for the fleet. As 'the eyes of the fleet,' seaplanes were expected to carry out traditional roles that had been pioneered by the Royal Navy in World War I. However, World War II proved to be the seaplane's swansong, its roles being usurped by high-performance aircraft operating from flight decks in numbers that were unthinkable in the prewar era. The Kingfisher, the last seaplane to serve at sea with the US Navy, came ashore in 1946.

Excluding the prototype ordered in March 1937 and which flew for the first time in the July of that year, a total of 1219 OS2U-1, -2 and -3 Kingfishers were built in the United States between 1938 and 1942. Noted for the first use of spot welding in the construction of a fuselage strong enough to withstand catapult launches, and for its full-span flaps, the Kingfisher was the first seaplane of monoplane design to enter American service. The first deliveries to the fleet

FAR LEFT: *Ensign P L Ferber flies his Vought-Sikorsky OS2U Kingfisher over amphibious assault forces as they approach the Pacific island of Angaur in the Carolines, September 1944. Ensign Ferber is engaged in ranging for the guns of the supporting warships – an important Kingfisher task.*

LEFT: *A Kingfisher, minus part of its engine cowling, is prepared for launch from the catapult on board a US warship, 1943.*

BELOW: *Kingfisher observation-scout floatplane in prewar colors. The float configuration is well shown.*

were made in August 1940, and establishment was standardized in time, with battleships embarking three seaplanes and cruisers four, the light cruisers of the 'Omaha' class being exceptional in that they embarked only two. Rather bizarrely, five destroyers were modified to carry a single Kingfisher apiece, losing their midships turret in the process, and as late as November 1943 two of these destroyers took their charges into action during the Marshalls campaign. The destroyer/seaplane combination, however, was not a happy one. The destroyer was too small to create the slick needed for successful recovery, while the 1500-gallon tank of avgas housed amidships on the upper deck represented an ultimately unacceptable hazard.

With a 450hp radial engine, the OS2U-3 Kingfisher was capable of a maximum speed of 264km/h (164mph) at 1677m (5500ft), had a range of 1457km (805 miles), and was able to carry either two bombs or two 159kg (350lb) depth-charges. It was used extensively by the US Navy, Coast Guard and Royal Navy for inshore antisubmarine patrols, its first (shared) success being off Cape Hatteras in July 1942. It was pressed into service as a bomber in the early stages of the Aleutians campaign, and in 1943, along with the Supermarine Walrus, it provided the only source of air power available to the Royal Navy in the Indian Ocean. But its chief claim to fame was in a role for which it was not primarily intended. As American forces fought their way into the western Pacific the Kingfisher was called upon to add air-sea rescue to its other duties, and in this role it saved many aviators shot down off enemy-held islands who otherwise would have been lost. Probably the most celebrated of its many rescues was off Truk on 10 April 1944 when a Kingfisher from the *North Carolina* saved first three and then a further seven ditched aviators, taxiing with her human cargo to a waiting submarine. Though the development of the helicopter foreshadowed the demise of the seaplane because of the loss of this role, the place of the latter was assured.

Vought-Sikorsky OS2U Kingfisher
Type: Single-engine maritime observation-scout.
Performance: Max speed 264km/h (164mph).
Service ceiling 3965m (13,000ft).
Range 1457km (805 miles).
Armament: Two 7.62mm (0.3in) machine-guns.

RIGHT: *A Supermarine Walrus II spotter-reconnaissance amphibian is hoisted aboard a British warship. Designed by RJ Mitchell, the Walrus entered service with the Fleet Air Arm in 1935, achieving fame as the first amphibian in the world to be catapulted from a warship with full military load. Despite its archaic appearance, the Walrus was still serving in FAA squadrons in 1945, mainly in the air-sea rescue role.*

BELOW: *A Kingfisher of the US Coast Guard flies over a merchant convoy on the lookout for enemy submarines. Note the depth-charge beneath the wing and the fixed 0.3in machine-gun in front of the pilot.*

ABOVE: *An Arado Ar-196 reconnaissance and coastal patrol floatplane, photographed aboard the German battlecruiser Gneisenau. Designed specifically for shipboard use, the Ar-196 had folding wings and a restricted range – 1078km (670 miles) – but was reasonably well protected by two 7.92mm machine-guns and a 20mm cannon (in the 'C' variant). First flown in the summer of 1937, little subsequent development took place and production was restricted to only 400.*

RIGHT: *A Kawanishi E7K 'Alf' reconnaissance seaplane of the Japanese Naval Air Force at the moment of recovery on board a mother-ship. Unusual in retaining a biplane configuration, the E7K was slow – a top speed of only 275km/h (171mph) – and vulnerable to interception, despite its armament fit of three 7.7mm machine-guns.*

TRANSPORT

ABOVE: *Douglas C-47 Skytrain transports deposit part of Major-General James M Gavin's 82nd US Airborne Division onto a drop-zone between Grave and Nijmegen in Holland, as part of Operation* Market Garden, *September 1944. The DZ has been marked with smoke, but the lack of ground activity implies that this is the first wave of assault troops to land. The 82nd went on to consolidate their landing areas and to seize the bridge at Nijmegen, but the British 1st Airborne Division at Arnhem to their north was not so fortunate.*

BELOW: *C-47s of the USAAF's Transport Command stand on a recently constructed runway in New Guinea, having brought in much-needed supplies to Allied forces fighting the Japanese, 1943.*

Air Transport
The Dakota

In American and British military service for more than two decades and still flying in considerable numbers in private hands at the present time, the Dakota's claim to have been a major contributor to Allied victory in World War II is hard to dispute. Indeed, such was its role in certain theaters known for their difficult terrain, most notably Burma and New Guinea, that it is probably not inaccurate to assert that the Dakota was the key to victory in these remote but important campaigns.

The association of Douglas transport aircraft and the American armed forces dates from 1934, when the US Navy acquired a single DC-2 airliner for service as a transport. Army Air Corps interest lagged behind that of the Navy but was more substantial, though in truth it could hardly have been less. It was not until 1936 that the AAC placed orders for DC-2s, and by that time the DC-3 had begun to enter service on US domestic routes. Despite an obvious and immediate interest in the newcomer, which extended to

taking possession of DC-3s in 1938; AAC did not place a production order with Douglas until 1940. Between 1936 and 1940 the AAC primarily concerned itself with bringing into service a number of DC-2/DC-3 hybrids and with setting down design specifications for a militarized DC-3. The most important of these requirements were the need for a double door and a strengthened floor, the AAC being anxious to secure two types of transport: a general-purpose aircraft that could carry freight as well as passengers and a personnel transport. As a result the DC-3 entered military service in two main forms: in October 1941 as the C-53 Skytrooper and in January 1942 as the C-47 Skytrain. They were essentially the same aircraft and were destined to fly under the shared designation of the Dakota: their only real difference was, as their names and the AAC specification suggests, that, lacking the Skytrain's strengthened floor, the Skytrooper could not carry cargo.

The Skytrain came in three basic forms, as the C-47, the C-47A

and the C-47B. There was very little in-service development of the aircraft, the C-47A being different from the C-47 only in that it incorporated a 24-volt electrical system in the place of the 12-volt circuits installed in the C-47. The C-47B differed from both by being fitted with two-stage superchargers, performance at high altitude being critically important for the 3100 aircraft built specifically for the China-Burma-India theater and for ferrying cargo from India to China over the infamous 'Hump' route. In its standard form as the C-47A, the Dakota had two 1200hp radial engines, a top speed of 370km/h (229mph) at 2287m (7500ft) and a range of 2414km (1500 miles) at an economical cruising speed of 298km/h (185mph) at 3050m (10,000ft). Normally unarmed, it could carry a maximum load of 4540kg (10,000lb) of cargo or a 2951kg (6500lb) personnel load, but in practice it was limited to a 2724kg (6000lb) cargo-load, 28 personnel or 18 stretcher cases and three medical personnel. It could embark a maximum of six parachute canisters and, most unusually for a transport, it had the means to carry two

spare propellers under the fuselage. Almost circular in cross-section throughout the length of its fuselage, the Dakota had a semi-retractable undercarriage.

The Dakota's first campaign predated American involvement in the war, the transport seeing service under British auspices in the course of the Iraq campaign in April 1941. With the outbreak of the Pacific War the Dakota was immediately involved in British operations in India and Southeast Asia and with American movements in the Pacific, but it was not until November 1942, in the course of the invasion of North Africa, that the C-47 saw service in the most photogenic of the roles that this workhorse of the skies was called upon to execute – the carrying of airborne forces into battle. The C-53 had to await the invasion of Sicily in July 1943 to make its debut in this role. With both aircraft able to tow gliders, the C-47 and C-53 were involved in every major airborne operation of the war after Sicily.

The Dakota's fame rests largely upon its worldwide service

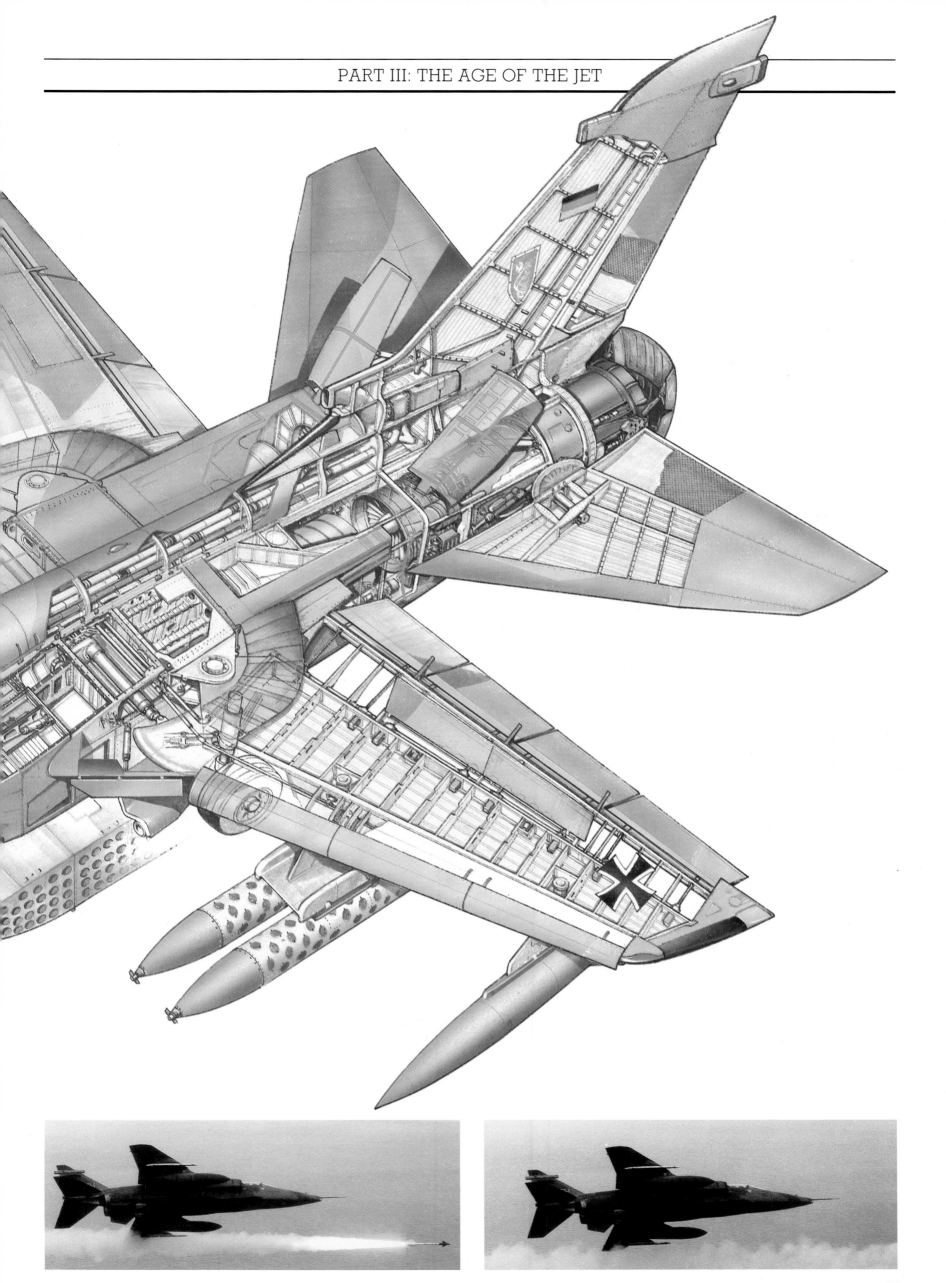

improved by advances in aerodynamics. An early breakthrough in this respect was the introduction of the swept-back wing, which the Americans and the Soviets applied to their North American F-86 Sabre and Mikoyan-Guryevich MiG-15 respectively after each superpower had profited from, and built upon, the pioneering work carried out by Germany during World War II. Another breakthrough came from streamlining to improve airflow at supersonic speeds, and yet another from the development of delta-winged aircraft, their maneuverability being further improved by the introduction of canard foreplanes. Perhaps the most celebrated of all innovations in the area of aerodynamics, however, was the development in the 1960s of the variable-geometry or 'swing' wing, a device enabled models such as the General Dynamics F-111 to combine in one aircraft the capacity to take off from and land on short runways, to undertake long-distance economical cruising and to fly at maximum speeds in excess of Mach 2: supersonic flight is facilitated by sweeping back the wings as far as possible; cruising and take off or landing are facilitated by reducing the angle of sweepback.

Innovations in propulsion systems and aerodynamics have been accompanied by less visible but equally important, if phenomenally costly, innovations in the sphere of avionics. In fact, there has been a veritable revolution in this sphere, reflected in increasingly advanced electronic systems for purposes such as navigation and target acquisition.

There has also been a revolution (of sorts) in the development of air weaponry. Many of the innovations – for instance, air-to-surface missiles (ASMs), cluster bombs and laser-guided bombs – have conferred greater striking power upon the 'armies of the air,' although the development of more sophisticated ground defenses, such as surface-to-air missiles (SAMs) and self-propelled anti-aircraft cannon, has tended to produce a countervailing effect, with the result that the balance between air power and antiaircraft ground defense has not necessarily tilted in favor of the former. Another innovation in air weapons systems, the air-to-air-missile (AAM), has affected not so much the balance between air power and ground defenses as that between rival forces in the air, enhancing as it does the ability of one aircraft to shoot down another.

But these innovations have not led to any fundamental change in air power roles, even if specialized missions such as inflight refueling, Electronic Warfare (EW) and Airborne Early Warning (AEW) have been added to them. During the modern age, as before, air power can be said to have six chief roles – the maintenance of airspace, strategic bombing, interdiction, close air support, reconnaissance and observation, and transport – although there have been certain shifts of emphasis, with expansion in some areas and decline in others.

Strategic bombing tends to fall into the latter category. Bombers have retained a certain utility, notably as a means of maintaining a nuclear deterrent posture, but bombing campaigns as such have, since the end of World War II, been few and far between. Indeed, the only air campaigns in modern times that came near to being 'strategic' were those mounted by the United States against North Vietnam between 1965 and 1973 – Operations 'Rolling Thunder' (March 1965-November 1968), 'Linebacker I' (May-October 1972) and 'Linebacker II' (December 1972). These campaigns, however, failed to live up entirely to the description. For one thing, they were carried out against a country that had hardly any strategic targets for the aircraft to hit – North Vietnam's war-making capacity was located, in effect, inside the Soviet bloc and China. Moreover, given that the United States practiced a considerable degree of restraint during these operations, the campaigns bore little resemblance to World War II style attempts to smash the enemy's will to continue the war. Linebacker II was perhaps an exception, President Nixon's chief aim being to bomb the North Vietnamese leaders back to the conference table.

Strategic bombing may have become a thing of the past, but there have certainly been a considerable number of interdiction campaigns since 1945 – i.e. campaigns in which air power has been

ABOVE: *Fairchild A-10 Thunderbolt II close support attack aircraft fly in formation, their unusual engine configuration clearly on view. With a maximum speed of only 681 km/h (423mph), it might be thought that the A-10 was a vulnerable aircraft in the modern age, but its task of close support to ground forces requires a degree of low-level accuracy not always available from a fast jet. The A-10's weapons fit is formidable.*

used to cut the enemy's immediate lines of supply and communication. During the Korean War (1950-53), for instance, the United States mounted sustained aerial attacks against targets such as roads, railways, bridges and supply centers so as to disrupt the North Korean and Chinese efforts to move reinforcements and supplies to the battlefront; these attacks were carried out by land-based aircraft such as the Martin B-26 Invader, the Boeing B-29 Superfortress and the Republic F-84 Thunderjet, as well as carrier-based aircraft such as the Grumman F-9F Panther. The United States mounted a similar, but much more extensive, air interdiction campaign during the involvement in Vietnam. At least two of the three bombing campaigns against the North – Rolling Thunder and Linebacker I – amounted in practice to interdiction campaigns, transportation lines being among the most important targets. At the same time, the United States carried out a massive interdiction campaign against the Ho Chi Minh Trail (1965-73), the aim being to

ABOVE: *Boeing B-52 Stratofortress heavy bombers of the US Strategic Air Command drop 454kg (1000lb) and 340 kg (750lb) conventional bombs onto targets close to Bien Hoa in South Vietnam, December 1966. As a single B-52 is capable of carrying up to 27,215kg (60,000lb) of bombs in an internal bay and on special wing pylons, the impact of a 'tactical' strike of this nature may be imagined.*

LEFT: *A Grumman F-14 Tomcat two-seat carrier-borne multirole combat aircraft comes in to land, its arrester hook extended. Most of the weapon hard-points are empty, but a single AIM-54 Phoenix missile may be seen beneath the fuselage. Fully armed, the F-14 can carry up to 6577kg (14,500lb) of assorted stores, including missiles.*

choke off the supply of men and material moving from the North to the South by way of Laos and Cambodia. As in Korea, the Americans used both land-based and carrier-based aircraft to sustain this twin interdiction effort, the aircraft involved including the Republic F-105 Thunderchief, the Douglas A-4 Skyhawk and the McDonnell Douglas F-4 Phantom. American strikes inflicted heavy damage on the Trail and the North Vietnamese homeland but, unfortunately for the attackers, the strikes failed to have any decisive effect on the outcome of the war.

Air power has also been used extensively in modern times to provide close support to forces on the battlefield. In Korea, for example, the United States and other Allied forces made strenuous efforts to provide close air support, carrying on in effect where they had left off at the end of World War II. Similarly, during the Arab-Israeli Wars of 1956, 1967, 1973 and 1982, the Israelis placed great emphasis upon air support; in 1956 and 1967 they used their air power in conjunction with their armor to conduct *blitzkrieg*-style campaigns in Sinai, although in the initial stages of the 1973 War they were forced to use their aircraft for a rather different purpose: that of fending off Egyptian and Syrian offensives. The provision of close air support has also been a feature of many counterinsurgency (COIN) campaigns, notably those conducted by the United States in Vietnam (1965-73) and the Soviet Union in

Afghanistan (post-1979). American ground operations in Vietnam invariably received air support, provided by fixed-wing aircraft such as the Douglas A-1 Skyraider, the North American F-100 Super Sabre and the F-4 Phantom, as well as by helicopter gunships such as the Bell UH-1D Iroquois and the Bell AH-1G Huey Cobra. The Soviet Union appears to have taken a page out of the American book, using aircraft such as the Mil Mi-24 Hind assault helicopter/helicopter gunship to cover its ground operations in Afghanistan.

Interestingly, both the Americans and the Soviets, in their respective campaigns, have placed heavy emphasis upon the helicopter for close support missions, a clear reminder that supersonic jets have their limitations in circumstances where pinpoint accuracy might well be necessary.

The helicopter has also been of great usefulness in the context of transporting men, equipment and supplies. At the tactical level, indeed, the helicopter has been much in evidence in the transport role, notably during the COIN campaigns waged by the French in Algeria (1954-62), the British in Borneo (1962-66) and South Arabia (1963-67) and the Americans in Vietnam. In all these cases the helicopter's 'go-anywhere' abilities proved invaluable, allowing the forces concerned to overcome many of the problems associated with fighting in rugged and inaccessible terrain. Indeed, the Americans based their tactics around the helicopter, using a lavish supply of such machines for the purposes of casualty evacuation, the rescue of any downed pilots and for airmobile operations in general.

The increasing use of helicopters for transportation has been matched by a steady growth in the use of fixed-wing aircraft in the same role, at tactical, operational and strategic levels. At the tactical level, for instance, the Americans used Lockheed C-130 Hercules for supply purposes in Vietnam; at the operation level, the

BELOW RIGHT: *A flight of Royal Navy Sea Harrier FRS-1 aircraft. Slightly modified forms of the Sea Harrier also serve with the Indian Navy.*
BELOW: *A Saab JA37 Viggen air defense interceptor of the Swedish Air Force banks to show its hefty weapons fit: on the outer wing hard-points and on either side of the center-line auxiliary fuel tank are AIM-9L Sidewinder air-to-air missiles, while on the inner wing hard-points are Sky Flash AAMs.*

Israelis used the same aircraft to good effect during their successful rescue mission to Entebbe in July 1976, while the Soviet Union used aircraft such as the Antonov An-12 Cub during its invasion of Afghanistan in December 1979. Fixed-wing aircraft have also been used extensively at a strategic level. For example, the Soviet Union used its air fleet to rush vast quantities of equipment to Egypt and Syria during the October 1973 Arab-Israeli War, to the pro-Soviet Popular Movement for the Liberation of Angola (MPLA) during the Angolan civil war (1975-76) and to the Ethiopian government during the Ogaden War (1977-78), transporting Cuban troops as well in the cases of Angola and Ethiopia. Similarly, the United States used its transport fleet to resupply Israel during the 1973 War, and also regularly practices the movement by air of troops earmarked to reinforce the Central Front in Europe.

There has also been an expansion during recent decades in the area of reconnaissance and observation, stemming in part from the fact that more effective reconnaissance technology has become available. The most dramatic aspect of modern aerial reconnaissance is the spy-satellite, but such devices have not become the only means, even at the strategic level. Both superpowers, in fact, have continued to deploy long-range, high-flying and fast strategic reconnaissance aircraft – the United States, for instance, has made good use of the Lockheed U-2 and more recently the Lockheed SR-71 Blackbird, which is reported to be able to fly at a speed of Mach 3 and at a height of 24,400m (80,000ft). Moreover, numerous air forces have continued to place great reliance upon tactical reconnaissance aircraft, although many of these have been recce versions of other types rather than purposebuilt machines: examples include Britain's English Electric Canberra PR and America's McDonnell RF-101 Voodoo, McDonnell-Douglas RF-4 Phantom and North American RA-5 Vigilante. Even so, recon-

naissance and observation has continued to rest very heavily upon the human eyeball – the man in the light airplane and helicopter. During the Vietnam War, for example, the Americans used strategic and tactical reconnaissance aircraft, but they also made continuous use of spotter planes and observation helicopters such as the Cessna O-1 Bird Dog and Hughes OH-6 Cayuse respectively; aircraft that proved to be invaluable for spotting enemy movements in the dense jungle below.

Given that in the modern age, as before, none of these air power roles can be effected without a greater or lesser degree of air superiority (even if only regionally), the maintenance of airspace has remained a vital task. Indeed, many states have given high priority to acquiring aircraft capable of denying airspace to potential or real enemies. In Korea, for instance, the Communists challenged American air power by deploying the highly effective MiG-15, but the United States responded with the introduction of the F-86 Sabre and thus maintained air superiority. Similarly, the North Vietnamese challenged American air power during the Vietnam War, fielding MiG-17s and MiG-21s, although in the event, most American aircraft losses came not from the MiGs but from the North's formidable antiaircraft defenses. The Israelis in June 1967 managed to gain air superiority on the first day of the 'Six-Day War' – by pre-emptive attack – and ruthlessly exploited airspace thereafter. The Six-Day War, indeed, offers a clear indication of the value of securing airspace and the decisive effects air power can have. The Vietnam War, on the other hand, shows that even a domination of airspace and a massive use of air power does not necessarily win wars. As this comparison demonstrates, the achievements of air power in the modern world have been somewhat mixed, but no one can deny that the aircraft has had a profound effect upon war at every level.

THE FIGHTER

Fighter Conflict in the Age of the Jet
The F-86 Sabre versus the MiG-15 in Korea

By the end of the 1940s both the United States and the Soviet Union had developed several makes of jet aircraft. These had been developed against a political background of rising tension between East and West. When Cold War hostility found expression in the Korean War (June 1950-July 1953) – with the United States making a massive contribution toward the United Nations cause and the Soviet Union sending weapons to the United Nations' adversaries – many of the aircraft in question were to be tested in combat. In consequence, Korea became the first conflict in which jet aircraft were used on an extensive scale. It also became the first conflict in which jet-versus-jet combat became a standard feature of air warfare, an innovation which took the form of a struggle for air supremacy primarily between the leading Soviet and American fighters of the time, the Mikoyan-Guryevich MiG-15 and the North American F-86 Sabre respectively.

The first of these rival jet fighters to appear in Korea was the MiG-15, which made its debut on 1 November 1950, shortly after the Communist Chinese had entered the war on the side of the North Koreans. Designed in the immediate aftermath of World War II, with an RD-45 engine based upon the British Rolls-Royce Nene 2 and swept-back wings based upon research captured from the Germans in 1945, the MiG-15 (NATO codename Fagot) soon proved itself superior to every Allied fighter then available in the theater of operations and, as such, gave the Allies a very

unpleasant shock. Responding to this threat, the United States in early December 1950 hurriedly deployed its leading fighter, the F-86 Sabre, an aircraft which had also been designed in the immediate aftermath of World War II and which also featured swept-back wings based on captured German research. Shortly afterward, on 17 December 1950, the MiG-15 and F-86 met for the first time in combat, over an area of northwestern Korea which American pilots were to nickname 'MiG Alley.' The outcome of this first clash was a victory for the US Air Force (USAF), the first of 792 MiG-15s claimed by Sabre pilots over the course of the next two-and-a-half years; 78 Sabres were to be lost during the same period.

This massive ten-to-one 'kill ratio' in favor of the Sabre appears to suggest that the MiG-15 was grossly inferior to its American rival, but this was not really the case. In some respects, in fact, the MiG-15 was superior to the Sabre, or at least to the version of the Sabre (F-86A) originally sent to Korea. It had a better rate of climb (nearly vertical), a greater operational ceiling and as good, if not better, maneuverability. It also had heavier armament and was faster at some altitudes, though these advantages were offset by the fact that it had a slower rate of fire and was marginally slower at most altitudes. On the debit side, however, it suffered the disadvantages of poor control at speeds above Mach 0.86 (which made gun aiming difficult), a lower rate of roll and directional instability at high altitudes. Thus in overall terms, allowing for strengths here and weaknesses there, the two rival fighters were fairly evenly matched. Only when the Americans deployed the F-86E (November 1951), which showed better control than its predecessor, and the F-86F (June 1952), which had a greater operational ceiling, a better rate of climb and a slightly higher speed, did the balance really tilt against the MiG-15.

LEFT: *A North American F-86A Sabre single-seat jet fighter, 1950. First flown on 1 October 1947, production versions of the F-86 began to reach front-line USAF squadrons in 1950, just in time for the Korean War.*
BELOW: *A Soviet-designed MiG-15 jet fighter in the colors of the communist Chinese. Its similarity to the F-86 is striking.*

The 'kill ratio' in favor of the Sabre was all the more impressive when one takes into consideration the fact that the American fighters were operating at the limits of their range capability. Indeed, as the Americans pushed deep into Communist territory in an attempt to secure airspace for their interdiction campaign, the Sabres reached the limits of their endurance, with the result that even with full internal fuel tanks and two 545-liter (20-gallon) drop-tanks the F-86A was restricted to only 20 minutes flying-time over the Yalu River; the MiGs that challenged them, by contrast, were operating from nearby bases, including a major base inside neighboring Manchuria (China) which was, for political reasons, 'off-limits' to United Nations' forces.

Moreover, the Communists held the tactical initiative, being able to attack (or not to attack) the incoming Sabres at their discretion, at a time and place of their choosing. They tried a number of different tactics, but generally favored the use of aerial ambushes, diving down from high altitudes (where the F-86A could not deal with them) in numbers ranging from just a few to several dozen at a time, to 'bounce' Sabre patrols; they made a special target of those running short of fuel and returning home. These methods brought the Communist pilots little success. The Americans responded effectively, devising tactics such as the 'jet stream,' whereby four flights of four Sabres entered MiG Alley at various heights – ranging typically from 8200m (27,000ft) to 10,000m (33,000ft) – at five-minute intervals and at high speed (Mach 0.87) so that if one flight were to be attacked the others could quickly converge and cover it; these flights operated in a 'fluid four' formation, with two element leaders each covered by a wingman.

These aerial battles down MiG Alley in many ways resembled the air battles of World War II. The aircraft doing the fighting were different, and the heights and speeds at which they flew could be different, but the tactics were often similar to those used during the

RIGHT: *A North Vietnamese MiG-17 is caught in the gunsight of an American F-105 Thunderchief, June 1967. The MiG has taken cannon fire in the starboard wing and is about to go down in flames. The MiG-17 (NATO codename 'Fresco') was an aerodynamically refined version of the MiG-15 which, when it first appeared in Soviet service in the 1950s, was a useful machine, capable of a top speed of 1145km/h (711mph) and armed with two 23mm NS-23 and one 37mm N-37 cannon, as well as hardpoints for a maximum of 500kg (1100lb) of stores. By the 1960s, however, it was becoming obsolete, and although the North Vietnamese pilots fought well, they were eventually outclassed by more modern American fighters. MiG-17s were used by Arab air forces in the fighter-bomber role in the Middle East Wars of 1967 and 1973.*

TOP, FAR RIGHT: *An F-86F Sabre flies over rugged terrain, Korea, 1950. The first Sabre unit to be deployed to Korea was the 4th Fighter Group (later retitled the 4th Fighter-Interceptor Wing), equipped with F-86As, and they soon encountered Chinese-piloted MiG-15s in the area to the south of the Yalu River known to the Americans as 'MiG Alley,' achieving a measure of superiority that was not to be lost. By 1951, the F-86 had been improved in the light of the lessons of air combat and once the 'F' variant had appeared, both operating altitude and maximum speed had been considerably improved, the former to 15,850m (52,000ft) and the latter to Mach 0.9 or 965km/h (600mph).*

BOTTOM, FAR RIGHT: *Soviet MiG-17s overfly a 'Skory'-class destroyer: a striking propaganda photograph from the 1950s.*

previous conflict and the *modus operandi* of the pilots had hardly changed – the pilots navigated by dead reckoning and map reading, sought out the enemy by peering out into the skies and attacked him by firing cannon. The outcome invariably depended upon pilot skill, something in which the Americans, by and large, enjoyed the advantage. Be that as it may, the pilots concerned could not have achieved consistent success without an effective fighter. They certainly found one in the Sabre, an aircraft that was to secure for itself, as a result of its success in Korea, a long career and a place in aviation history.

MiG-15 *bis*

Type: Single-seat fighter.
Performance: Max speed 1076 km/h (668mph) at 12,000m (39,000ft).
Service ceiling 15,500m (51,000ft).
Range: 1424km (885 miles).
Armament: one 37mm (1.5in) NS-37 cannon and two 23mm (0.9in) NS-23 cannon (later versions had two NR-23 revolver cannon instead of NS-23s); underwing hardpoints for slipper tanks or up to 500kg (1100lb) of stores.

North American F-86A Sabre

Type: Single-seat fighter.
Performance: Max speed 1086km/h (675mph).
Service ceiling 15,240m (48,000ft).
Range: 740km (460 miles).
Armament: Six 12.7mm (0.5in) Colt Browning M-3 guns and two underwing hardpoints for tanks or pods carrying 454kg (1000lb) of stores.

Developing the Jet Fighter
The MiG-21 Fishbed

Until the appearance of the MiG-25 Foxbat at the beginning of the 1970s, Western air forces believed, almost as an article of faith, that in terms of respective aircraft they held a very considerable technological lead over their Soviet bloc opposite numbers. Given this belief, it followed that they were convinced that such aircraft as the Mikoyan-Guryevich MiG-21 Fishbed was qualitatively inferior to such contemporary aircraft as the Lockheed F-104 Starfighter, its direct American equivalent. This, in all probability, was the case, but the fact that the MiG-21 remains in production, and is very likely to remain in service at least with non-Warsaw Pact countries into the 21st century, strongly suggests that it was endowed with a stamina unsuspected by Western observers in the 1960s. Though in-service development has transformed the Fishbed, three decades of employment in various air forces have shown that the basic MiG-21 aircraft was sound in concept and design, while the numbers in which it has been built – in excess of 10,000 – has inevitably conferred upon it the characteristic best summarized by the old adage that quantity has a quality all of its own.

The MiG-21 was developed directly as a result of combat experience in the Korean War. Like the Starfighter, the MiG-21 was the response to the demand for a small, lightweight 'air superiority' fighter, and with the Fishbed Mikoyan-Guryevich developed an aircraft that was even smaller than Lockheed's product but one that was at least the equal of the Starfighter in terms of handling and maneuverability. The Soviet aircraft, however, sacrificed everything to the needs of combat performance and was built around the minimum armament, two 30mm (1.2in) cannon, needed to account for an enemy fighter. It was inferior to the Starfighter in terms of range, flexibility, weapons load and avionics. Moreover, although somewhat simplistic, the Fishbed was not a simple aircraft, despite the fact that it did represent a cost-effective investment. After entering service in 1958 as a day interceptor, however, in-service development, in large measure the result of major Soviet advances in avionics technology, has substantially changed the appearance of the Fishbed and enabled it to operate in a number of roles. Although it remains primarily a low-level tactical air-defense fighter, working in partnership with the much larger MiG-23

BELOW: *A MiG-21MF (NATO codename 'Fishbed-J') of the Soviet Air Force: the most common variant of the 1960s.*
TOP RIGHT: *An earlier version of the MiG-21 – the 21F ('Fishbed-C') – shown in Yugoslav colors.*
BOTTOM RIGHT: *An Egyptian MiG-21 goes down in flames, a victim of Israeli ground fire close to the Suez Canal during the later stages of the October 1973 'Yom Kippur' War.*

Flogger, improvements have conferred upon it a limited all-weather capability, a light strike role and the ability to conduct reconnaissance missions. In these roles, and as a trainer capacity, the Fishbed is certain to see out the 1980s in Warsaw Pact service.

The in-service development program of the MiG-21 has encompassed a bewildering number of variants which are impossible to chronicle separately here but which have extended across four main production serials and two quite distinct phases. In the first of these phases, which lasted into the early 1970s, development was characterized by piecemeal change. From the MiG-21F

RIGHT: *Soviet pilots discuss the finer points of tactics as they walk past their Sukhoi Su-17 single-seat attack and close support aircraft. The Su-17 (NATO codename 'Fitter-C') has a maximum speed of Mach 2.2 or 2305km/h (1432mph) and is armed with two 30mm NR-30 cannon, as well as underwing pylons capable of carrying up to 4000kg (8818lb) of stores.*

BELOW: *A Libyan Su-22 'Fitter-J' photographed by a US Navy aircraft. The Su-22 is an export version of the Soviet Su-17 but with reduced equipment standards. This aircraft is carrying two AA-2 Atoll air-to-air missiles.*

FAR RIGHT: *A Saab Viggen fighter of the Swedish Air Force. The prototype Viggen first flew in 1967 and the aircraft was one of the first to employ canard foreplanes.*

onward, the Fishbed was subjected to improvements of engine, armament, fuel capacity and avionics, but the net result of these changes was an increase of weight and dimensions, and hence total area and resistance, that could not be continued without adversely affecting overall performance. Because, even with larger engines, the later versions of the Fishbed were equipped with a relatively small powerpack, the increase in the size of the aircraft's cross section (caused by the enlarging of the engine intakes and by the widening of the dorsal spine in order to accommodate more fuel and equipment) ensured that with the appearance of the MiG-21MF the limit of development within the existing airframe had been reached. Development, therefore, moved into a second, more radical phase, the result being the MiG-21 *bis*, which represented as great a qualitative advance over the MiG-21MF as that aircraft had been over the MiG-21F. Entering service in 1976, the MiG-21 *bis* has a silhouette and capabilities that betray its ancestry, though it is larger and heavier than its predecessors. With an overall weight of 10,000kg (22,000lb), an engine producing 7500kg (6500lb) of thrust, a top speed of 2125km/h (1320mph) at 11,000m (36,000ft), the MiG-21 *bis* has a maximum range of 1760km (1100 miles) and an effective combat radius of 500km (300 miles). An internally mounted twin-barrelled 23mm (0.9in) cannon allows the MiG-21 *bis* to carry a centerline drop tank in addition to a mixed ordnance load under the wings. The MiG-21 *bis* is able to operate

with up to 1500kg (3300lb) of weapons, the usual armament for the air-defense role being two AA-2-2 Advanced Atoll and two AA-8 Aphid air-to-air missiles.

First exported to non-Warsaw Pact countries in 1963, the MiG-21 has been made under license in China, Czechoslovakia, India and, apparently, North Korea. It has seen service in the air forces of 26 nations outside the Warsaw Pact, but despite its numbers and quite respectable performance figures at all stages of its career, its combat record has not been impressive. A partial explanation of its relative failure lies in the fact that in the major wars in

which it has fought, the MiG-21 has found itself pitted against much superior aircraft flown by aircrew and air forces far superior to those operating the Soviet product. In service with the Egyptian, Syrian and Iraqi air forces in 1967, it had no opportunity to show its qualities after the pulverizing Israeli attack that announced the start of the Six-Day War, and in the 1973 conflict its piecemeal commitment against a rampant Israeli Air Force resulted in heavy losses for no corresponding return. Similarly, it was employed too infrequently and in too small numbers by the North Vietnamese to register success against American fighters in the course of the war

RIGHT: *A BAC Lightning F.6 single-seat all-weather interceptor fighter of No 11 Squadron, RAF, comes in to land at RAF Valley, November 1981. First flown in August 1964, the F.6 has a top speed of Mach 2.1 or 2230km/h (1386mph) and is normally armed with two Red Top air-to-air missiles and two 30mm Aden cannon.*

LEFT: *An Israeli Kfir C-2 fighter, First flown in 1973, the Kfir ('Lion Cub') is capable of a top speed of Mach 2.3 or 2440km/h (1516mph).*

BELOW LEFT: *A MiG-23 'Flogger-E' fighter armed with AA-2 'Atoll' air-to-air missiles. The 'Flogger-E' is the export version of the 'Flogger-B,' one of the earliest variants produced for Soviet service.*

BELOW: *The USAF employs F-5 fighters, painted in Soviet colors, in its combat training programs.*

in Vietnam; but even in Indian service in 1971, during the war that resulted in the creation of Bangladesh, the MiG-21 appears to have recorded very few kills, although it seems to have performed adequately against a numerically inferior and, for the most part, defensively minded Pakistani Air Force.

Despite its lack of success in these wars, however, the MiG-21 is likely to remain an attractive buy for many Third World countries and, as a result, is all but certain to have fresh opportunities to redeem its rather indifferent reputation. In prestige terms it provides a genuine Mach 2 capability, without the often daunting sophistication of Western aircraft, and it remains a cheap product in comparison with Western alternatives. But having failed to record any clear-cut success to date, the MiG-21 is unlikely to do so in the future and its impact in future conflicts is likely to be no more than marginal.

ABOVE: *A McDonnell Douglas F-18 Hornet single-seat carrier-borne multirole combat aircraft being prepared for launch, August 1985.*

TOP RIGHT: *A two-seat training version of the F-16 Fighting Falcon in Danish Air Force service. The F-16 serves with the air forces of Belgium, Holland and Norway as well as with the USAF.*

RIGHT: *A cutaway drawing of an F-18 Hornet of US Marine Squadron VFA-125. It is armed with AIM-9L Sidewinder and AIM-7F Sparrow AAMs and Walleye TV-guided 'smart' bombs.*

The MiG-21MF
Type: Single-seat jet fighter.
Performance: Max speed 2070km/h (1285mph) or Mach 2.1. Service ceiling 18,000m (59,050ft).
Range 1800km (1118 miles).
Armament: 23mm (0.9in) machine cannon, with provision for two AA-2 Atoll air-to-air missiles.

GROUND ATTACK

Close Support to Forces on the Ground
The F-100 Super Sabre and the Bell AH-1G Attack Helicopter

The United States formally committed her ground forces to South Vietnam in early 1965, and from that time until she ended her military involvement there in January 1973, Allied ground forces in Vietnam received massive support from the air on a continuous basis. During the whole of this period, in fact, there was hardly a day when Allied air forces – the United States Air Force (USAF), the United States Navy (USN), the United States Marine Corps (USMC), the United States Army, or the South Vietnamese Air Force – were not in action providing close air support (CAS) to forces on the ground. An indication of the scale of this massive support can be gauged from the fact that at the height of the American involvement in the war on average some 800 sorties a day were being flown by the tactical air forces alone.

The aircraft used to provide such support ranged across a broad spectrum. At one end was the giant, eight-engine Boeing B-52 Stratofortress, which, despite its original status as a strategic bomber, was used during the Vietnam War mainly as an interdiction and close air support aircraft; flying in from bases in Guam and Thailand, the B-52 dropped its huge bomb-loads from great heights on targets such as infiltration routes, suspected enemy base camps and troop concentrations, including those around Khe Sanh in early 1968. At the other end of the spectrum were light, piston-engine machines such as the Cessna O-1 Bird Dog, a Forward Air Control (FAC) aircraft charged with the task of spotting enemy

LEFT: *A Bell AH-1S Huey Cobra antiarmor attack helicopter, equipped with launchers for eight Hellfire laser-seeking antitank missiles and a nose-mounted 20mm M197 three-barrel gun. This is the latest version of the Cobra.*
BELOW: *A North American F-100 Super Sabre single-seat fighter-bomber drops its bombs onto Viet Cong positions in South Vietnam, June 1967.*

LEFT: *Bell AH-1S Huey Cobra helicopters of the Japanese Defense Force, armed with launchers for eight TOW (tube-launched, optically tracked, wire-guided) antitank missiles and 2.75in rocket pods. The nose-mounted 20mm gun may also be seen.*

BELOW: *A cutaway of a Hughes AH-64 Apache battlefield helicopter, armed with Hellfire laser-seeking antitank missiles and 2.75in rocket pods, as well as a 30mm Hughes Chain Gun. The helicopter's sensor package is mounted in the nose, something which is now seen as a drawback as the pilot has to leave cover to acquire his targets.*

movement on the ground and directing fire, whether from other aircraft or artillery, upon enemy positions. In between these contrasting types were numerous fighter-bombers, specialized support aircraft such as modified transport planes, and purposebuilt helicopter gunships.

The most important CAS fighter-bomber of the war was the North American F-100 Super Sabre, nicknamed the 'Hun' (from its designation F-100). The better-known McDonnell-Douglas Phantom II was also used extensively in the CAS role, but as combat sortie figures for 1969 illustrate – the Phantom made 19,185 sorties while the Super Sabre made 52,699 – the F-100 was responsible for more close support sorties than the Phantom, or, for that matter, any other single aircraft type. It was a role in which the 'Hun' excelled, although like other fast jets the F-100 was too blunt an instrument to deploy in some circumstances, notably when the enemy used 'hugging' tactics, moving in close to friendly forces so as to discourage the Allies from calling in an air strike.

Fortunately for Allied ground forces, the Americans could also call upon the services of slower aircraft able to achieve greater accuracy – notably the assault helicopter. Indeed, the Americans throughout their involvement in Vietnam made good use of attack helicopters, so-called gunships. Initially the rotary-winged equivalent of the F-100 was the Bell UH-1 Iroquois or 'Huey,' which was used both as a troop carrier and as a fire-platform or gunship. By late 1967, however, the Huey was being replaced in the latter role

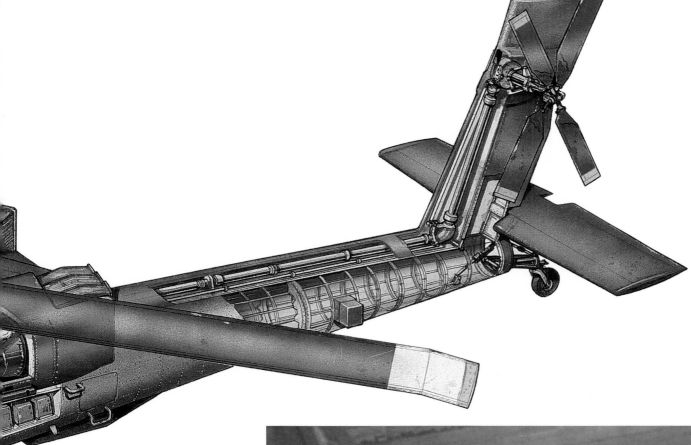

ABOVE: *A Fairchild A-10 Thunderbolt II single-seat close support aircraft of the 75th Tactical Fighter Squadron, 23rd Tactical Fighter Wing, aggressively painted, stands at dispersal at its home base of England AFB, Louisiana, October 1986. In the center of the 'shark's teeth' may be seen the barrel of the 30mm GAU-8/A cannon, while beneath the wings hang a variety of stores, including Maverick (left) and Walleye (right) air-to-surface missiles. The A-10 has a total of 11 weapons pylons, capable of lifting a total of 7257kg (16,000lb) of stores – a mixture of free-fall bombs, cluster-bomb units and laser- or TV-guided bombs. The AGM-65B Maverick TV-guided ASM has a range of approximately 19km (12 miles), and is locked onto the target by the A-10 pilot.*

BELOW: *A North American F-100 Super Sabre fighter-bomber prepares to attack Viet Cong positions with high-explosive bombs and napalm, 1966.*

ABOVE: *A Northrop F-5A Freedom Fighter of the US 4503rd Tactical Fighter Squadron drops its bombs on a Viet Cong position, 1966. Although useful as a lightweight ground-attack aircraft, the F-5A did not see widespread service in the USAF.*

LEFT: *A Douglas A-4E Skyhawk of the US Navy's Attack Squadron VA-23 drops a 454kg (1000lb) bomb over South Vietnam, October 1965.*

RIGHT: *Close-up of a 30mm GAU-8/A cannon, fitted to an A-10 Thunderbolt II attack aircraft. This seven-barrel Gatling-type gun can deliver armor-piercing or high-explosive ammunition at the rate of 2100 or 4200 rounds a minute.*

FAR RIGHT: *McDonnell-Douglas F-4 Phantom II fighter-bombers of the US Navy's Fighter Squadrons VF.111 and 51, from the carrier USS Coral Sea, drop bombs on North Vietnam, August 1972.*

by the Bell AH-1 or Huey Cobra, a faster, well-armed 'chopper,' purposebuilt for the attack role. The Huey Cobra soon proved itself to be a formidable machine, able to direct its awesome firepower with great accuracy against enemy forces, and able to take considerable punishment from enemy ground fire. In time, it came to symbolize American CAS missions in Vietnam as much as the F-105 Thunderchief came to symbolize Operation Rolling Thunder and the B-52 Stratofortress Operation Linebacker II.

North American F-100D Super Sabre
Type: Single-seat fighter-bomber.
Performance: Max speed at 11,000m (36,000ft), 1390km/h (864mph).
Service ceiling 15,250m (50,000ft).
Range 885km (550 miles).
Armament: Four 20mm (0.8in) cannon, each with 200 rounds; up to 3402kg (7500lb) of ordnance on underwing pylons.

Bell AH-1G Huey Cobra
Type: Two-seat attack helicopter.
Performance: Max speed 352km/h (219mph).
Range 507km (315 miles).
Armament: Single six-barrel 7.62mm (0.3in) 'minigun' on early version; later version carried either two 'miniguns' with 4000 rounds each or two 40mm (1.6in) grenade launchers with 300 rounds each, or one 'minigun' and one grenade launcher, plus external stores under wing stubs, including 70mm (2.75in) air-to-ground rockets, 7.62mm (0.3in) machine-guns or 20mm (0.8in) cannon.

The Israeli Pre-emptive Strike, 5 June 1967
The Dassault Mirage III

On the eve of the Arab-Israeli 'Six-Day War' of June 1967, the balance of forces between Israel and her immediate Arab adversaries, Egypt, Syria and Jordan, seemed to rest heavily in favor of the latter. The Israelis were numerically inferior in terms of military manpower (by a ratio of 1:1.5), tanks (1:2), aircraft (1:3) and artillery (1:8), leading some observers to predict that, even allowing for compensating factors such as superior fighting spirit and technical expertise, the Israelis would be hard-pressed to survive. Such predictions proved, in the event, to be mistaken, for the Israelis not only survived but also achieved a tremendous victory over their Arab opponents. That they did so stemmed in large measure from

their ruthless exploitation of air supremacy, which they had achieved on the first day of the war by launching a pre-emptive air strike that shattered the Arab air forces on the ground.

Israeli air strength just prior to this strike stood at about 300, of which about 200 were fighters or strike aircraft. The most modern plane in the Israeli inventory was the French-built Dassault Mirage IIICJ, which equipped three squadrons, while the balance consisted of one squadron of Dassault Super Mystère B2s, three squadrons of Dassault Mystère IVAs, two squadrons of Dassault Ouragans, one squadron of Sud Vautours and some 70 Fouga Magister training/light attack aircraft. The Israelis decided to use

ABOVE: *Dassault-Breguet Mirage III multirole fighters of the Israeli Air Force, photographed on a training mission, March 1967. First flown in November 1956, the Mirage III went on to become a significant aircraft of the modern age. With a maximum speed of 1390km/h (863mph) and an armament fit which included two 30mm DEFA cannon as well as pylons for up to 1362kg (3000lb) of stores, it offered a capability and potential which the Israelis needed to counter the new Soviet equipment being delivered to neighboring Arab powers in the mid-1960s. On 5 June 1967, the Mirages showed their prowess when they acted as protectors of the Mystère and Super Mystère attack aircraft as they carried out their devastating pre-emptive strike against Arab airfields.*

LEFT: *An Israeli Mirage III, put on display in the aftermath of the October 1973 'Yom Kippur' War. This particular aircraft has victory symbols for eight Egyptian machines, shot down in the air battles over the Suez Canal. In 1973, the Egyptians were using MiG-21s, but the Mirages were able to cope well, particularly when flown by experienced Israeli pilots. Such battles could only take place, however, after the Israelis, with American technological help, had evolved countermeasures to the Soviet-supplied antiair 'umbrella' of surface-to-air missiles and radar-controlled cannon which protected the Arab forces.*

RIGHT: *The scene in the immediate aftermath of the Israeli pre-emptive strike on 5 June 1967: three Egyptian MiG-21s lie completely destroyed, and the surrounding runway is blackened by fire. All three seem to have received direct hits from bombs or rockets: a tribute to the accuracy of the Israeli pilots. The way that the aircraft are parked in a neat row also illustrates the complete surprise achieved on 5 June, when a total of at least 240 Egyptian aircraft were destroyed. Hardly surprisingly, this was something which the Egyptians were determined to avoid in the future. In the period after June 1967, with Soviet help, they initiated a process of building hardened shelters for their aircraft and deployed antiair defenses around their airfields.*

FAR RIGHT: *A Mirage fighter in Australian colors, armed with three Paveway laser-homing bombs. Once the target has been illuminated by a laser, the bombs will travel along the beam, achieving an impressive degree of accuracy. These particular weapons appear to be 907kg (2000lb) GBU-15 CWW variants: they can be carried by most types of tactical aircraft.*

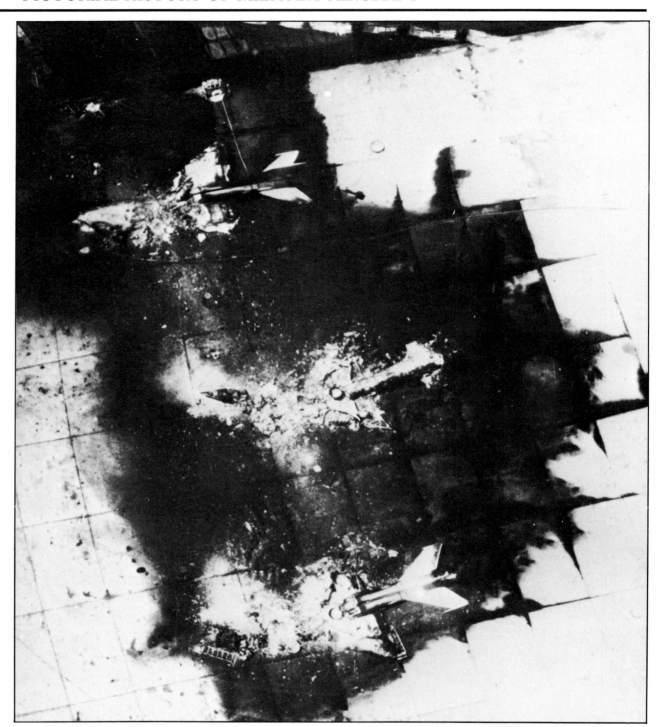

all these types, with the exception of the Magisters, to put in the pre-emptive strike. The main recipient was to be Egypt which, because of its strength of manpower, armor, artillery and aircraft – some 450 first-rank combat planes – was regarded by the Israelis as the chief threat to their security. They gave priority to destroying Egypt's bomber fleet, comprising three squadrons of Ilyushin Il-28s and two squadrons of Tupolev Tu-16s, and to her air-superiority fighters, six squadrons of MiG-21s.

In their planning for the pre-emptive strike, the Israelis gave particular attention to the timing of the first attacks. They decided against commencing at dawn, preferring instead to attack at 08.45 hours Egyptian time (07.45 hours Israeli time), by which time Egyptian air patrols would have landed, interceptors on ground alert would have been stood down, and the early-morning mists over

the Nile Delta would have cleared. They also made strenuous efforts to ensure that their attacks would be synchronized, no easy task considering that the aircraft concerned had varying cruising speeds and would be flying off from several bases. As to the question of flight paths, the Israelis decided that aircraft assigned to attack airfields in Sinai would fly directly from Israel, those attacking airfields in Upper (southern) Egypt would fly down the Gulf of Aqaba and the Red Sea, and those earmarked to attack bases in the Nile Delta would sweep out over the Mediterranean and then move in over the Egyptian coastline. The planners

BELOW: *An Egyptian MiG-17 fighter-bomber makes a low-level strafing run over an Israeli column in Sinai, June 1967. Not all Egyptian aircraft were destroyed in the pre-emptive strike.*

ABOVE: *An Italian Aermacchi MB-339C Veltro 2 light attack aircraft, equipped with AIM-9 Sidewinder AAMs, gun-pods and rocket launchers. MB-339s were used by the Argentinians in the Falklands War of 1982.*

LEFT: *A Hawker Siddeley/British Aerospace Hawk two-seat advanced trainer, converted to the air-defense role by the addition of underwing AIM-9 Sidewinder AAMs.*

RIGHT: *An Argentinian-built FMA IA-58A Pucara counter-insurgency (COIN) attack aircraft, captured by the British in the Falklands and given RAF markings. It carries two 20mm cannon and four 7.62mm machine-guns.*

allocated the four major airfields in Sinai to the Mystères and Ouragans, the main Nile Delta airfields to the Super Mystères and Mirages and the airfields in Upper Egypt to the twin-engine Vautours. All attacking aircraft were to fly at extremely low altitude throughout, so as to avoid detection by enemy radar systems deployed to protect the airfields.

Meticulous planning was matched by brilliant execution. Flying in at extremely low level, the Israelis achieved complete surprise as they cratered enemy runways with special bombs and strafed enemy aircraft parked or taxiing below them. The Israelis kept up these attacks for over an hour, sending in wave after wave of aircraft, each wave having 10 minutes in the target vicinity before giving way to the next wave and then returning to base to rearm and refuel; an amazingly fast 'turnaround time' of only seven minutes, plus a serviceability rate of 90 percent, meant that the Israelis managed to keep virtually all their strike forces in action during this critical period.

The net result of these attacks was that within two hours or so the Israelis had destroyed over 240 (possibly as many as 300) enemy aircraft, effectively decimating the Egyptian Air Force. Later on 5 June, as Egypt's allies entered the war, the Israelis extended their attacks to airbases in Jordan and Syria, wiping out

Jordan's small air force and effectively crippling Syria's. Thus the Israelis destroyed the Egyptian, Syrian and Jordanian air forces, and lost only 20 of their own planes in the process. To all intents and purposes, they now ruled the skies over the Middle East, and their Magisters and other aircraft could provide unrestricted support to advances by their ground forces in Sinai, the West Bank and the Golan Heights. The pre-emptive strike had been an enormous gamble – if the Arabs had chosen to attack Israeli cities, only 12 aircraft would have stood in their way – but in the event it paid off handsomely, proving to be one of the most decisive uses of air power in aviation history.

Dassault Mirage IIICJ

Type: Single-seat interceptor and tactical strike aircraft.
Performance: Max speed 1390km/h (863mph) at sea level, 2230km/h (1386mph) at altitude.
Service ceiling 17,000m (55,775ft).
Range: 1200km (746 miles).
Armament: Two 30mm (1.2in) DEFA cannon plus external pylons for up to 1362kg (3000lb) of ordnance.

Air Defense
The SAM 'Umbrella' of 1973
and the Israeli Response

If Israel's victory in the June 1967 'Six-Day War' stemmed essentially from her seizure and exploitation of air supremacy, her initial setbacks during the subsequent Yom Kippur War in October 1973 owed much to the fact that during the opening phase of the latter conflict she was denied air supremacy, in the immediate battlefield area, by her Egyptian and Syrian enemies. The Israelis had few problems in terms of air-to-air combat – during the course of the October 1973 War they claim to have shot down 370 Arab aircraft, losing only four of their own in dogfights – but they did have great difficulties, during the early stages of the war at least, in countering Egyptian-Syrian antiaircraft defense systems. Indeed, when the Israelis tried to use their air power to stem the Arab advances on the Golan and Sinai fronts, they found that their pilots were greeted by a wall of cannon fire and missiles sent up by the Syrian and Egyptian air defenses on these fronts.

The Israelis had received a foretaste of this problem during the closing stages of the 'War of Attrition,' which began in earnest in the spring of 1969 with Egyptian artillery attacks across the Suez Canal, and ended in August 1970 with both sides accepting an American-sponsored ceasefire. As the Egyptians stepped up their attacks against Israeli positions, the Israelis responded by launching commando raids, artillery bombardments and, above all, by mounting air strikes against targets on the west bank of the waterway and also, from January 1970, against targets in the vicinity of Cairo. In mounting these air strikes, the Israelis were able to brush aside Egyptian air and ground defenses, but when the Soviet Union (then Egypt's ally) installed new air defense systems around the capital and within some 20km (12 miles) of the Suez Canal, the equation began to change. Indeed, as the Israelis intensified their attacks against Egyptian positions along the Canal (deep penetration strikes were abandoned so as to avoid confrontation with the Soviet Union), they began to suffer serious losses – seven aircraft were lost during July 1970 alone – and had to work out new

ABOVE: *A Grumman E-1 Tracer (right) and a Grumman E-2A Hawkeye in flight. The Hawkeye superseded the Tracer in the airborne warning role with the US Navy from the mid-1960s and the E-2C version remains in service.*
LEFT: *Soviet air defense troops prepare an SA-3 (NATO codename 'Goa') medium-altitude SAM: a missile with a range of 29km (18 miles).*
BELOW: *SA-3 SAMs mounted on the back of a ZIL-157 truck. Each SA-3 system includes 'Flat Face' target acquisition and 'Low Blow' target-tracking and missile guidance radars.*

tactics to deal with the Soviet-installed surface-to-air missiles (SAMs) and antiaircraft (AA) gun defenses. Whether these losses would have continued to mount must remain a moot point, since both sides agreed to a ceasefire in the following month. However, when conflict resumed on 6 October 1973, heralded by a joint Egyptian-Syrian offensive on the Sinai and Golan fronts respectively, the Israelis were to feel the full effects of the Soviet-installed SAM and AA systems. For by the time the war began, both the Egyptians and the Syrians had set up sophisticated air-defense systems on their respective fronts, air 'umbrellas' that were to provide their advancing armies with cover against Israeli air attack during the opening phase of the war.

These air-defense systems consisted of SAMs designed to provide cover against aircraft flying at high-to-medium altitude (SA-2), medium-to-low altitude (SA-3 and SA-6, the latter being mounted on a tracked vehicle), and low altitude (manportable SA-7), these missiles being backed up by the self-propelled, radar-directed ZSU-23-4 cannon. The system was thus an integrated one, providing defense at all altitudes. The Israelis, having been on the receiving end of some of these missiles during the War of Attrition, were not oblivious to the threat they faced. In fact, they had marked down SAM batteries and radar sites as priority targets in the event of another round of war with the Arabs. When war came, however, the Israelis did not get the chance to implement these plans, since with their ground forces reeling back under the weight of the Syrian-Egyptian advance, they had to give priority to providing close-air support to their hard-pressed army. The consequences, for the Israeli Air Force, were disastrous. As they flew in to offer air support, they suffered heavy losses to the Arab air-defense systems, losing 40 aircraft, 30 Skyhawks and 10 Phantoms – during the first afternoon of the war.

This contest between the Arab defense systems and the Israeli strike planes did not, however, remain one-sided for long. Like the Americans over North Vietnam in 1972, the Israelis developed ways of coping with the threat. One method was to take evasive action, maneuvering the 'cold' side of the aircraft towards a heat-seeking SAM. Another was to change the angle of attack, for instance by carrying out a steep diving attack against the SA-6 so as

to exploit that particular missile's low angle of trajectory at launch. Yet another was the use of electronic countermeasures (ECM), ranging from the use of 'chaff' (strips of metal or fiberglass released to confuse radar) to sophisticated jamming techniques employed by special ECM aircraft. By using measures such as these, the Israelis gradually fought back against the Arab air defenses, thus offering better support to their ground forces, which in turn opened up gaps in the Arab air-defense systems as they recovered the initiative and advanced. In fact, the Israeli Air Force had begun to establish mastery over the SAMs to such an extent that, including the initial heavy losses, the Israelis achieved a lower aircraft loss rate per sortie during the October 1973 War than they had during that of June 1967.

The Israelis had managed to develop a highly effective response to the air-defense systems and this was confirmed beyond question when they undertook an invasion of Lebanon in June 1982 (Operation Peace for Galilee). In order to cover the invasion, the Israelis needed to dispose of the numerous SAM batteries (mainly SA-6) the Syrians had installed in the Beqa'a Valley. In the event, the Israelis were able to overcome these systems with consummate ease, the basis of their success being the coordinated use of electronic warfare (EW) aircraft, remotely piloted vehicles (RPVs), antiradiation missiles and conventional 'iron' bombs. They used EW aircraft such as converted Boeing 707s to identify missile site radars, RPVs to locate the SAM batteries and act as decoys (as soon as the Syrians tracked the RPVs, they revealed the location and frequency of their radar) and strike aircraft, protected by ECM equipment and directed toward the SAMs by Grumman E-2C Hawkeyes, to take out the SAM radars (by firing AGM-45 Shrike antiradiation missiles) and the SAMs themselves (by dropping conventional bombs). Thus the Israelis succeeded in neutralizing the Syrian SAM threat, demonstrating that air-defense systems were not, despite the predictions of some observers after the Yom Kippur War, invincible. For all that, however, the package worked out by the Israelis is unlikely to remain immutable, for just as air-defense systems have been weakened by countermeasures, so the latter have been undermined to some extent by counter-countermeasures. The cycle is not likely to end yet.

ABOVE: *A Soviet SA-2 (NATO codename 'Guideline') SAM, captured by the Israelis, is set up on an American firing range. The SA-2 is perhaps the most widely used of all SAMs, having been deployed against the Israelis since the mid-1960s and having been encountered by the Americans over North Vietnam. It is normally carried to its launch site on the back of a trailer towed by a ZIL-151/157 or a ZIL-131 truck, from which it is pulled backward onto a large rotatable launcher. Backed by a radar system known to NATO as 'Fan Song,' the missile has a range of about 50km (31 miles).*

ABOVE LEFT: *An American aircraft, remotely controlled for the purposes of a test, is approached by a surface-to-air missile.*

RIGHT: *A British Aerospace Rapier low-level air-defense missile system at the moment of firing. The system, first produced in 1971, comprises a fire unit, optical tracker and generator, although early in 1983 the British Army took delivery of newly developed Tracked Rapier systems, designed to provide battlefield mobility. The static Rapier did well in the Falklands War, once its radars had recovered from the rigors of a sea voyage.*

AIRMOBILITY

TV week

November 20 – November 26 / 1988

Star Tribune

Vanna White/
She portrays the legendary love goddess Venus in the
NBC movie "The Goddess of Love"/**Page 5**

With day-by-day listings
for broadcast and cable

Davy Crockett returns to TV

By Jay Bobbin
Tribune TV Log

Few characters in TV history have staked their claim to fame by wearing a coonskin cap, but the most famous one is about to return.

Immortalized in a theme song as the "king of the wild frontier," Davy Crockett was first played by Fess Parker on the 1950s "Disneyland" series. He was in only six episodes and was killed off in the third. The subsequent stories recalled exploits earlier in his life, and that is the same technique being used in the "Davy Crockett" revival that will begin Sunday on NBC. It is one of the four "wheels" that make up the network's "Magical World of Disney" anthology. (Another of them, multi-episode adaptation of the movie "The Absent-Minded Professor," premieres next Sunday.)

Crockett is played by youthful Tim Dunigan, seen last season on the syndicated show "Captain Power and the Soldiers of the Universe." An older Davy Crockett also is featured in the initial two-hour story. Parker was to play the part, but the Disney studio's initial agreement with him couldn't be negotiated, so Johnny Cash appears as the older Crockett.

Although many youngsters will be getting their first exposure to Crockett through Dunigan's portrayal, the actor has some childhood memories of the characters. "I was very, very young when the original shows aired," Dunigan said , "but I thought it was just the greatest thing in the world that my cousin had an authentic coonskin cap.

"My remembrances of Fess Parker are based more on the 'Daniel Boone' series he did in the 1960s, which was more a part of my own adolescence. Still, at that age, I couldn't make a distinction between his playing Crockett and his playing Boone. To me, he was just the guy who always wore the coonskin cap and was out in the woods with the Indians," Dunigan said.

"Fess Parker is always going to be Davy Crockett to a certain group of people, no matter what I do, and I hope that he is."

Conversion grid

Cable stations may appear on different channels in each local cable system. This chart lists the stations and what channels they appear on in the major local cable systems.

	Anoka	Apple Valley	Bloomington	Col. Heights	Eagan/Burns.	Fridley	Hastings	Lake Mtka.	Minneapolis	North Central	Northwest	Roseville	St. Louis Park	St. Paul	Shakopee	S. Wash. Co.	Southwest	Wash. County	White Bear
Am. Movie Classic			27		25									53	51				
Arts & Ent. (AEN)	21	C16	16	21	21	35	47	16	16	21	26	21	35	16	28	51	16	49	21
BET				48						27	39	48		27			27		69
BRAVO (BRV)	45			45	45		17		50	45	53	45		52		27	50	26	45
C-Span	28	Q30	30	28	28	43	27	30	30	28	30	28	32	30	40	50	30	52	28
C-Span II	38			38	38				31	38	31	38		31			31		38
CBN Cable Network	18	L25	28	18	18	28	28	32	52	18	7	18	31	36	34	52	52	48	18
Cable News (CNN)	3	3	3	3	3	3	19	33	3	3	3	3	27	3	45	49	3	45	22
CNN Headline	14	B15	15	14	14	15	45	15	15	14	15	14	30	15	37	43	15	40	14
Cinemax (MAX)	43	X37	48	43	43			40	35	48	43	50	43	50	24	28	48	23	43
CVN		O28						21	28						18		28		
Discovery (DSC)	31	I22	22	31	31	10	25	43	22	31	22	31		22	39	35	22	51	31
Disney (DIS)	42	D17	45	42	42	22	23	39	18	42	49	42	21	51	21	46	18	28	42
ESPN (ESN)	10	10	7	10	10	7	51	10	7	10	10	10	28	7	50	34	7	42	15
Eternal Word	49		25	49	49		33		54	49	61	49		56	36	36			49
Fashion									24						10	22	24		
Festival (FES)																			
Fin. News (FNN)	22	K24	24	22	22	24	41	24	24	22	24	22	15	24	33	47	24	43	33
HBO	37	1	49	37	37	20	52	37	14	37	47	37	14	47	23	23	14	27	37
Home Shopping			18			38	18						18	42		55	18		
KARE-TV (NBC)	11	11	11	11	11	11	11	11	11	11	11	11	11	11	11	11	11	11	11
KITN-TV (UHF 29)	29	P29	29	29	29	29	8	29	29	29	29	29	34	29	7	8	29	8	29
KMSP-TV	9	9	9	9	9	9	9	9	9	9	9	9	9	9	9	9	9	9	9
KSTP-TV (ABC)	5	5	5	5	5	5	5	5	5	5	5	5	5	5	5	5	5	5	5
KTCA-TV (PBS)	2	2	2	2	2	2	2	2	2	2	2	2	2	2	2	2	2	2	2
KTCI-TV (PBS)	17	F19	17	17	17		7	17	17	17	17	17	7	17	8	7	17	7	17
KTMA-TV (UHF 23)	23	J23	23	23	23	23	32	23	23	23	23	23	36	23	41	18	23	32	23
KXLI-TV (UHF 41)	39	U34	41	39	39	19		34	41	39	41	39	26	41	52	41	41	41	39
LBN									50	54					36		33		
Learning Ch. (LRN)	48			48	48		34	28			48	53	48	58	26	33		47	48
Lifetime (LIF)	30	G20	20	30	30	18	43	14	20	30	20	30	33	20	27	37	20	36	30
Music TV	7	T33	40	7	7	27	36	25	40	7	14	7	24	40	30	45	40	55	7
Movie Channel (TMC)	41	Z39	47	41	41	14	30		47	41	51	41	19	49	17	30	47	31	41
Nashville (NSH)	20	H21	21	20	20	20	42	27	20	21	20	25	21	31	26	38	21	35	20
Nickelodeon (NIK)	32	M26	26	32	32	26	49	31	26	32	27	32	23	26	48	26	44		32
Nostalgia (NOS)									24	37						24	37	24	
PTL	49			49			37		0		49	49			21	0	21		49
QVC	19			19	19		26			19	18	19		37	19	26		25	19
Showtime (SHO)	40	7	46	40	40	16	20	41	46	40	48	40	16	48	20	25	46	30	40
TBS-TV	12	8	8	12	12	8	48	7	8	12	12	12	17	8	47	40	8	37	12
Tempo (TEM)	55		55	67			46		25	65	52	65		46	49	44	25	46	65
TNT	44	E18	14	44	44	17		44	36	44	28	44		28			36		44
Travel	27	F19		27	27				51	27	44	27		57			51		27
Trinity (TBN)									1	61					35		1		
USA	24	12	12	24	24	12	33	12	12	24	16	24	20	12	25	20	12	19	24
Univision				66					57	54	68	54		43		31	54		62
Video Hits 1	26	S32	38	26	26	30	21	26	38	26	40	26		38		39	38	39	26
WCCO-TV (CBS)	4	4	4	4	4	4	4	4	4	4	4	4	4	4	4	4	4	4	4
WCCO-II (CCO)	8		8	8			44		39	8	8	8			44	42	39	34	8
WCCO Weather	15	V35	42	15	15	37	35		53	15	19	15	13		13	17	53	17	16
WGN-TV	13	13	13	13	13	13		13	13	13	13	13	29	13	29	32	13		13
WOR									22	10						32	10	20	
Weather Channel	50	W36	39	50	50	36		51	36	50	38	50	12	14	38		51		50

Vanna White plays Venus

By Jay Bobbin
Tribune TV Log

She is the most famous letter-spinner in history, but Vanna White is aiming to prove that she has other abilities, too.

One of television's most recognizable personalities, thanks to her role on the game show "Wheel of Fortune," she is about to have her first major acting role. White, who has appeared as herself in a number of series and specials, plays Venus in "The Goddess of Love," Sunday's new NBC TV movie, which brings the mythical beauty back to life after she has been encased in stone for 3,000 years.

She proceeds to complicate the life of an engaged-to-be-married hairdresser (David Naughton), who jokingly suggests that Venus is the bride he really wants. Among the others involved are his actual fiancee (Amanda Bearse) and his business partner (rock star Little Richard).

"For the past six years I've been turning letters on 'Wheel of Fortune,' and most of America doesn't even know that I can talk," White said. . For two hours, though I get to talk and act in this movie. It's a fantasy, it's fun and it's lighthearted, and I think my fans will appreciate and accept that."

As saturated as the public has been with White's wholesome, smiling image in recent years, she said, "I think this is perfect timing for 'The Goddess of Love,' because I've laid low lately. There was a period last year when I seemed to be on the cover of every magazine, or when there was an article on me in every publication. (There also was a much-promoted autobiographical book, 'Vanna Speaks.') Quite frankly, I got sick of seeing myself . . . so I knew that America was tired of it, too. I thought it was time to take a break from the press.

"Since then I did this movie, and it's time to get going again and to tell people, 'Hey, I'm doing something new. I hope you like it.' A lot of people are going to wonder, 'Can she do it? Can she pull it off? Is it going to be good or bad?' I just hope everybody will be pleased with it."

White can afford to appear a bit campy in "The Goddess of Love,"

Vanna White

since the script reflects that tone. "Although it's a lighthearted comedy," she said, "it was hard to sit there and say something like, 'Where dost thou slumber?' My dialogue throughout this whole thing is very difficult, and to pull it off as if it was my normal style of language was hard.

"Venus comes to life in the 1980s to find out what true love is, and when she's used to saying all her 'thees' and 'thous' — then she's suddenly in a time when everybody is really hip — it's a major change for her."

Established though "Wheel of Fortune" is, some changes are being worked into the program..

The biggest change is yet to come, though: While he will remain with the hugely successful nighttime version, host Pat Sajak

will leave the NBC edition soon, because he will begin his own late-night talk show for CBS in January. At press time a new host had yet to be selected, but whatever the outcome, Vanna has no plans to pack her bags.

"I don't know how much input I'll have," she said about her role in the selection of Sajak's daytime 'Wheel' replacement, "but I'm sure they'll narrow it down to a few people, then put them on camera with me to see how I work with them. I think a lot will depend on how I look with the other person, how we interact, and things like that."

White has a contract to continue with "Wheel" through 1992, and that appears to suit her just fine. "It has been very good to me," she said, "and I will be very good to it."

Sports action/ Broadcast

Sunday/ November 20/1988

Noon

⑪ **NFL Football**/Indianapolis Colts at Minnesota Vikings

3:00pm

④ **NFL Football**/Philadelphia Eagles at New York Giants

⑤ **Golf**/Merrill Lynch Shoot-Out Finals from Ventana Canyon, Tucson, Ariz., tape delay

Monday/ November 21/1988

8:00pm

⑤ **NFL Football**/Washington Redskins at San Francisco 49ers

Thursday/ November 24/1988

11:30am

④ **NFL Football**/Minnesota Vikings at Detroit Lions

3:00pm

⑪ **NFL Football**/Houston Oilers at Dallas Cowboys

Friday/ November 25/1988

1:30pm

④ **College Football**/Alabama vs. Auburn From Birmingham.

8:30pm

㉙ **College Hockey**/Minnesota vs. Colorado College From the Air Force Academy.

Saturday/ November 26/1988

9:30am

⑨ **High School Football**/Minnesota Nine-Man State Championship from the Metrodome.

10:30am

㉙ **Women's College Vollyball**/Illinois vs. Minnesota, tape delay

Noon

⑨ **High School Football**/Minnesota Class C State Championship from the Metrodome.

1:00pm

⑪ **Bowling**/Budweiser Classic from Columbus, Ohio, tape delay

1:30pm

④ **College Football**/Florida State vs. Florida

2:30pm

⑤ **College Football**/Notre Dame at USC

⑨ **High School Football**/Minnesota Class B State Championship from the Metrodome.

⑪ **Golf**/Skins Game, Front-Nine Play from PGA West, La Quinta, Calif.

5:00pm

⑨ **High School Football**/Minnesota Class A State Championship from the Metrodome.

7:00pm

㊶ **NHL Hockey**/Minnesota North Stars at Toronto Maple Leafs

7:30pm

④ **NBA Basketball**/Los Angeles Lakers at Detroit Pistons

7:35pm

⑨ **High School Football**/Minnesota Class AA State Championship from the Metrodome.

8:30pm

㉙ **College Hockey**/Minnesota vs. Colorado College from the Air Force Academy.

Cable/

Sunday/ November 20/1988

1:00pm

[CCO] **College Volleyball**/Indiana at Northwestern

5:00pm

[ESN] **Golf**/Senior PGA Machado Ford Classic, final round from the Key Biscayne (Fla.) Golf Club, tape delay

6:30pm

[CCO] **NHL Hockey**/New Jersey Devils at Philadelphia Flyers

7:00pm

[ESN] **NFL Football**/New England Patriots at Miami Dolphins

Monday/ November 21/1988

Noon

[ESN] **CFL Football**/Western Division Semifinal, tape delay

8:00pm

[ESN] **Figure Skating**/1988 Skate America: Women's Competition from Portland, Maine, tape delay

Tuesday/ November 22/1988

7:05pm

[TBS] **NBA Basketball**/Los Angeles Lakers at New York Knicks

8:00pm

[ESN] **Boxing**/Ras-I Aluja Bramble vs. Bryant Taden, lightweights from Atlantic City.

Wednesday/ November 23/1988

6:00pm

[ESN] **College Basketball**/Big Apple NIT, first semifinal from Madison Square Garden.

Airmobility
The Bell UH-1 Iroquois Helicopter

During the First Indochina War (1946-54), French forces found great difficulty in mounting mobile operations against the Communist Viet Minh guerrillas, a problem that stemmed essentially from the rugged nature of the terrain – for the most part mountain and jungle – and from the fact that the French had to rely on motor transport (at best) to conduct such operations. Some 20 years later, when the Americans began formally to send ground forces to Vietnam, they too faced the problem of moving across seemingly impenetrable terrain but, with the passage of time, technological developments seemed to provide an answer. The helicopter, still in its infancy at the time of the First Indochina War, had now come into its own, offering an alternative means of movement in a land of mountains, jungle and rivers.

From the very outset of their involvement in South Vietnam, in fact, the Americans came to regard the helicopter as the key to cross-country mobility, an indispensable means of evacuating casualties, supplying bases and ferrying troops into and out of the inhospitable and inaccessible terrain that characterizes much of South Vietnam. Indeed, America's main tactic during the first three years of the war, that of 'finding, fixing and destroying' the enemy (also known as 'search and destroy'), became dependent upon the availability of helicopter transports, since operations of the search and destroy variety very often had to be mounted against outlying areas dominated by the enemy. The widespread use of the chopper entailed heavy costs, particularly as these machines were vulnerable to ground fire when landing or taking off, and when flying at low level, but against this the helicopter provided the Americans with a degree of mobility that would otherwise have been impossible to achieve.

As far as transport was concerned, the most widely used helicopter was the Bell UH-1 Iroquois, known affectionately as the

LEFT: *Bell UH-1 Iroquois utility helicopters approach a US firebase in South Vietnam, 1967. The UH-1, known as the 'Huey' from the sound of its designation, was a major part of the 'airmobility' concept in Vietnam, being used to carry troops and supplies into enemy-infiltrated areas to set up protected firebases, and to ensure the bases were sustained.* BELOW: *The door gunner on a UH-1 lays down suppressive fire from his 0.3in machine-gun, Mekong Delta area, 1967.*

'Huey' (because of its original service designation UH-1). Other helicopters too were used for logistical purposes, including the Boeing-Vertol CH-47 Chinook, but the task of light transport (and that of fire support until the arrival of the Bell AH-1G Huey Cobra in late 1967) fell primarily to the Huey, in its several variants. The first version to serve in Vietnam was the UH-1A, which had room for four passengers. Produced in small numbers only, this version was supplanted by the UH-1D, which featured an extended cabin for up to 14 troops (or six litters and a medical attendant), and by the UH-1H, which had a more powerful engine than the 'D.'

Between them, the UH-1D and the UH-1H accounted for the bulk of the US Army's assault transport capability in Vietnam, and the sight of these helicopters landing troops in jungle or mountain terrain became a familiar one to many people in the West. Huey helicopters have also served with over 70 air forces worldwide, more than any other military aircraft since World War II.

Bell UH-1H Iroquois

Type: Utility and transport helicopter.
Performance: Max speed fully loaded 204km/h (127mph). Range 512km (318 miles).
Armament: One or two door-mounted 7.62mm (0.3in) M60 machine-guns; or, in gunship versions, fixed, forward-firing 7.62mm (0.3) machine-guns, 7.62mm (0.3in) 'minigun' multi-barrel machine-guns, 20mm (0.8in) cannon 40mm (1.6in) grenade launchers and pods of 70mm (2.75in)rockets.

ABOVE: *An Aerospatiale/Westland SA-330 Puma medium transport helicopter of the Commonwealth Monitoring Force in Rhodesia/ Zimbabwe passes over Victoria Falls, 1980.*
FAR LEFT: *A Sikorsky CH-54 Tarhe heavy-lift 'flying crane' helicopter of the US Army helps in the dismantling of a pontoon bridge. The advantages of such lift capability are substantial.*
BELOW: *A Sikorsky CH-53 Sea Stallion heavy lift transport/assault helicopter of the US Navy in flight: the largest and most powerful such machine in the West.*

The Attack Helicopter and its Development
The Mil Mi-24 Hind

In much the same way as the Bell AH-1G Huey Cobra helicopter gunship came to epitomize American close air-support missions in South Vietnam, so one particular helicopter, the Mil Mi-24 (NATO codename Hind) has come to symbolize Soviet close-support missions in Afghanistan. Indeed, the Hind appearing suddenly over the crest of a hill and unleashing a salvo of rockets against Afghan guerrillas has become a familiar sight on Western television screens, and has developed into a classic image of the Soviet Union's counterinsurgency campaign in Afghanistan.

However, to liken the Mi-24 to the Huey Cobra would be in many ways misleading. True, both have performed as gunships, but whereas the Huey Cobra was specifically designed to fulfill such a role, the Hind was designed as a multirole combat helicopter, capable of carrying a squad or perhaps a section of infantry and of acting as a tank-killer as well as performing in the ground-attack role. As such, it is much larger and heavier than the Huey

Cobra, measuring 17m (55ft 9in) in length and 4.25m (14ft) in height, and has an empty weight of 6500kg (14,000lb), more than twice that of its American counterpart. Despite its size and weight, however, the Hind is a very fast machine, capable of reaching a maximum speed of 320km/h (200mph) and a cruising speed of 260km/h (160mph). It is powered by two Isotov turboshafts, 1500shp in the early models and 2200shp in the later models.

The Mi-24 first entered service in the early 1970s, the original version being the Hind-A. This version was followed by the Hind-C (the Hind-B did not enter service), the Hind-D (in 1975) and, more recently, the Hind-E. All these versions are capable of acting as troop carriers, having cabin room for at least eight infantrymen, and all are heavily armed, two pylons for rocket pods and a pair of rails for antitank missiles on each stub wing being common to all versions except the 'C,' which has no provision for the antitank missiles. Common features notwithstanding, the Hind-D and Hind-E

BOTTOM LEFT: *Soviet Mil Mi-24 (NATO codename 'Hind-D') tactical gunship helicopters, deployed in a wintry setting.*

RIGHT: *A Hind-D is prepared for action, showing its hefty armament fit to advantage. Under the nose is the remote-control turret housing a 12.7mm four-barrel gun for use against ground or air targets, while beneath the wings may be seen UV-32-57 pods for 57mm rockets. Not shown are the outer wing pylons for AT-6 'Spiral' antitank missiles.*

BELOW: *Troops rush to board a Hind-D in East German service, entering the helicopter through the fuselage door. The Hind was designed to carry a squad of fully armed assault infantry, supported by helicopter fire.*

ABOVE: *US troops deploy from a Boeing-Vertol CH-47 Chinook medium transport/assault helicopter during an operation in South Vietnam, 1966.* BELOW: *A dramatic study of the US Army's AH-64 Apache attack helicopter.*

versions are in several respects an improvement on the earlier models. Not only do they have more advanced avionics, notably new all-weather sighting systems, but they have a redesigned canopy (which affords the pilot and weapons operator a better view), bullet-proof windows, better armor protection for the crew and, in terms of enhanced firepower, more formidable nose-mounted guns to supplement the standard array of external weapons – the Hind-A has a 12.7mm (0.5in) machine-gun in the nose and the Hind-C no nose gun at all, whereas the Hind-D has a four-barrel 14.5 or 20mm (0.6 or 0.8in) cannon and the Hind-E a 30mm (1.2in) cannon with its own laser target-seeker. Thus the 'A' and 'C' versions might best be described as assault helicopters, while the 'D,' 'E' and perhaps the even more recent Hind-F (capable of carrying six antitank missiles) might best be described as helicopter gunships, although of course all versions are capable of performing to a greater or lesser degree as both armed troop carriers and gunships. In its various sub-species, then, the Hind is an extremely versatile aircraft, and one that provides its users with a great deal of tactical flexibility.

Indeed, if a NATO versus Warsaw Pact war were to break out in the near future the Soviet Union would probably use the Hind liberally, exploiting its possibilities as a fire platform, tank buster and armed troop carrier. In such an eventuality, the Hind would probably be a valuable asset to the Warsaw Pact, though this must remain a moot point since such circumstances have not arisen in Europe. However, the Hind has seen combat in Afghanistan, and in

this conflict it has already demonstrated its worth as an assault helicopter and as a gunship; it has allowed Soviet forces to attack Afghan guerrillas on mountain slopes, thus relieving the problem of crowning the heights, and to land troops suddenly in inaccessible areas, so easing the problem of operating inside a country with poor communications. The Hind's record in Afghanistan has not, however, been uniformly impressive. A large and heavy helicopter, it has proved ungainly and hence vulnerable to ground fire, even to relatively light 12.7mm (0.5in) antiaircraft machine-guns. It may well be, therefore, that while being able to perform several different roles adequately, the Hind is perhaps too cumbersome to carry out individual tasks as effectively as a specialist helicopter.

Mil Mi-24 Hind

Type: Assault helicopter and gunship.
Performance: Max speed 320km/h (200mph).
Cruising speed 260km/h (160mph).
Service ceiling 5500m (18,000ft).
Range 900km (559 miles).
Armament: Up to four pods each containing 32 57mm (2.2in) rockets, plus up to four antitank missiles, on stub wings; 12.7mm (0.5in) machine-gun in nose (Hind-A and -C). 14.5mm (0.6in) or 20mm (0.8in) cannon in nose turret (Hind-D), 30mm (1.2in) cannon in nose turret (Hind-E).

ABOVE RIGHT: *Mi-8s in Egyptian colors deploy troops to a forward base during a joint US-Egyptian exercise, 1982.*

RIGHT: *A Messerschmitt-Bölkow-Blöhm Bö-105 attack helicopter of the West German Army armed with TOW antitank missiles.*

BOMBING

The Bombing of North Vietnam

The F-105 Thunderchief, the F-4 Phantom II and the B-52 Stratofortress

The American bombing campaign against North Vietnam was carried out intermittently for over eight years. The Americans launched their first attacks against the North on 5 August 1964, but then declined to mount any more until February 1965, when further strikes were conducted under the codenames Flaming Dart and Flaming Dart II. Then, at the start of the following month, began a sustained bombing offensive codenamed Operation Rolling Thunder, lasting until 1 November 1968. Finally, after an interval of more than three years, the Americans resumed their offensive under the new codename Freedom Train, an operation superseded in the following month by Linebacker, which lasted until January 1973. Thus the bombing campaign took the form not of one continuous offensive, like those conducted against Germany and Japan during World War II, but rather of several operations of varying duration.

The air campaigns against North Vietnam also differed from those against the Axis powers in being much less indiscriminate. The Americans dropped a heavier tonnage on North Vietnam than they had on either Germany or Japan – 860,000 tonnes during Rolling Thunder alone – but they were much more circumspect as to where they dropped the bombs, attempting as far as possible to avoid heavy civilian casualties. This inhibition can be attributed in part to humanitarian motives but perhaps more importantly to a desire to minimize domestic and international hostility to the bombing. Whatever the main cause, however, such inhibitions colored the United States' approach to a greater or lesser extent throughout the entire campaign. Indeed, far from conducting a deliberate, systematic and all-out strategic bombing campaign, the Americans acted in many respects with remarkable restraint.

This was particularly true of the period between 2 March 1965 and 1 November 1968, when the Johnson administration, after authorizing comparatively minor retaliatory strikes in August 1964 and February 1965, directed sustained bombing attacks against the North under Operation Rolling Thunder. The latter, despite the heavy tonnage of bombs dropped, was not a genuine strategic bombing campaign. Admittedly, the architects of this offensive had calculated that by bombing the North they could force the Hanoi government to call off its aggression against the South. But they had also calculated that a short, sharp all-out offensive designed to smash the North's entire military and economic infrastructure would be politically unwise – particularly as heavy civilian casualties might result – and militarily unnecessary. They decided, therefore, that the United States should adopt a gradual approach, using air power sparingly to begin with and intensifying the attacks only if Hanoi refused to see the error of its ways.

This decision to refrain from launching a campaign of mass destruction was reflected in the fact that the Americans chose to hold back their strategic bombers, the Boeing B-52 Stratofortresses (which were used mainly over South Vietnam and the Ho Chi Minh Trail), preferring instead to use tactical air power against the North. Indeed, the vast majority of air strikes against the North were carried out not by B-52s but by tactical aircraft such as the Douglas A-4 Skyhawk and Grumman A-6 Intruder, which operated mainly from aircraft carriers in the Tonkin Gulf, the McDonnell-Douglas F-4 Phantom II, which saw service primarily with the Navy

LEFT: *A photograph taken over a practice target shows a General Dynamics F-111D interdiction/strike aircraft dropping twelve 227kg (500lb) bombs from its tandem triplet wing mountings. The 'D' variant experienced some problems in service.*
BELOW: *Republic F-105F Thunderchief tactical strike aircraft, equipped with electronic countermeasures pods.*

and the Air Force, and above all the Air Force's Republic F-105 Thunderchief, which operated out of bases in Thailand. The Thunderchief, originally designed to mount tactical nuclear strikes but pressed into service as an 'iron' bomb carrier, came to symbolize the entire Rolling Thunder offensive, mounting some 75 percent of American strikes against the North. As a strike aircraft, the 'Thud' proved highly reliable, although its true potential was never realized because of the numerous targeting restrictions placed upon American pilots by their own government.

From the very outset of the Rolling Thunder offensive, in fact, the Johnson administration imposed a whole series of limitations and restrictions that tended to deaden the impact the bombing might otherwise have made. In addition to the general rule that civilian areas should be avoided whenever possible, pilots were ordered to leave North Vietnam's main ports and urban areas (notably Hanoi and Haiphong) alone, as well as the country's air-defense system, and to stay out of the area adjacent to the border with China. When the Johnson administration discovered that Hanoi remained unwilling to talk peace, it lifted certain of these restrictions, allowing its forces to retaliate against air defenses (August 1965), to strike POL (petrol, oil, lubricant) facilities and powerplants in Hanoi and Haiphong (June 1966) and to attack key

LEFT: *The RF-4C version of the Phantom is the USAF's standard tactical reconnaissance aircraft. It is normally unarmed and carries a range of sensor equipment, including cameras, infrared linescan and radar.*

BELOW LEFT: *An RAF Phantom FGR Mark 2 of No 23 Squadron stands ready at Mount Pleasant airfield, Port Stanley, East Falkland, armed with AIM-9 Sidewinder air-to-air missiles.*

BELOW: *An Israeli F-4E comes in to land, deploying its colorful drag-chute. It is equipped with extra fuel tanks and ECM pods, and is fitted with a refueling probe on the starboard side of the fuselage top.*

communications targets inside the Hanoi-Haiphong area (July 1967). Even so, most of the worthwhile strategic targets remained 'off-limits' throughout the offensive.

As well as having to operate within the confines imposed upon them by their own government, American pilots had also to contend with restrictions of geography, notably the annual monsoon (October to March), which tended to interfere with air missions, and the terrain – jungle, forests and mountains for the most part – which tended to complicate the problem of locating targets. Then again, restrictions of a sort were placed upon American pilots by the enemy, who with Soviet and Chinese assistance built up a formidable air-defense system consisting of antiaircraft (AA) guns, surface-to-air missiles (SAMs) and MiG fighters, originally MiG-15s and -17s, and, from December 1965, MiG-21s. Flying over North Vietnam was no picnic, as many American pilots discovered to their cost. By the time the government called off Rolling Thunder, on 1 November 1968, 938 aircraft had been lost over the North.

Unfortunately for the pilots concerned, this sacrifice proved to be in vain. Despite a gradual increase in the number of sorties, and in the scope of the bombing, the Hanoi government showed no signs during 1965, 1966 or even 1967 of abandoning its struggle against the South. In fact, the North Vietnamese proved to be much more resilient and determined than Defense Secretary Robert McNamara had calculated, and by early 1968 the US administration was beginning to have second thoughts about its bombing offensive. Concluding that the military and political costs of Rolling Thunder were outweighing the benefits, the Johnson administration proceeded in April 1968 to suspend all bombing attacks north of the 19th parallel, in the hopes that Hanoi would respond by entering into peace negotiations. On 1 November 1968, after a signal from Hanoi that the North Vietnamese were willing to talk, Johnson called off the bombing completely.

The Americans then switched the main thrust of their attacks to the Ho Chi Minh Trail, but some three-and-a-half years later, after

LEFT: *A Tupolev Tu-22M strategic attack and reconnaissance aircraft (NATO codename 'Backfire'), with an AS-4 'Kitchen' air-to-surface missile slightly recessed beneath the fuselage.*

RIGHT: *Crew members 'scramble' toward their waiting Boeing B-52 Stratofortress long-range heavy bomber. Nuclear-armed B-52s of the US Strategic Air Command are on alert at all times.*

BELOW RIGHT: *The most recent addition to the US strategic armory is the B-1B bomber. This aircraft has been designed to have as small a radar 'signature' as possible. The B-1B can reach a maximum speed of Mach 1.25 and a range of 7500 km (4600 miles).*

BELOW, FAR RIGHT: *A B-52H, equipped with two underwing Hound Dog missiles.*

BELOW: *An FB-111A of the USAF. The FB-111 is the strategic bombing version of the F-111. In this role the FB-111 can carry nuclear armed AGM-69 SRAMs (Short Range Attack Missiles) as well as free-fall bombs.*

the North Vietnamese invasion of the South on 30 March 1972, President Richard Nixon authorized the resumption of strikes against the North. These attacks were initially limited to areas up to 40km (25 miles) north of the Demilitarized Zone (DMZ), but by mid-April the area of operations had been extended to the 20th parallel. On 8 May, after peace talks had broken down again, the attacks were extended even further, a narrow buffer strip along the border with China being the only part of North Vietnam declared 'off-limits.' Operation Linebacker, America's second sustained bombing offensive against North Vietnam, was now underway.

The rationale behind Linebacker – to reduce North Vietnam's capability to wage war against the South and to make Hanoi seek a peace settlement – was not markedly different from that behind Rolling Thunder, but the chances of succeeding were now more favorable. For one thing, the North Vietnamese were more vulnerable to interdiction attacks, because, having switched to a strategy of conventional war, they required a much more elaborate logistical chain than had previously been the case when they favored guerrilla infiltration. Second, the North Vietnamese no longer enjoyed the benefit of 'sanctuaries' (areas in which

American pilots were forbidden to operate) because Nixon, unlike his predecessor, placed fewer restrictions upon American mission directives. Third, the North Vietnamese no longer enjoyed the respites that had been provided by inaccurate American attacks against targets such as bridges, because the US forces were now equipped with 'smart' weapons such as Paveway laser-guided bombs (LGBs), which would be delivered with pinpoint accuracy onto targets illuminated by laser beam. All in all, therefore, the Americans were confident of success, although North Vietnam's formidable air defenses – a veritable arsenal of AA guns and SAMs, backed by over 200 MiG fighters – posed a threat that could not easily be discounted.

In the event, American pilots were well satisfied with the results they achieved. They overcame the North's air defenses through the use of strike 'packages' – large air formations consisting not only of strike aircraft but also of fighters, so as to defend against MiG interception; electronic countermeasures (ECM) carriers, for radar jamming; 'Wild Weasels,' for seeking out SAM sites; flak-suppression planes and other types such as reconnaissance and command aircraft. The attack role, and reconnaissance and SAM seeking, were usually carried out by F-4 Phantoms, which by this time had replaced the Thunderchief as the Americans' premier fighter-bomber. The attacks inflicted severe damage upon North Vietnam's supply network and infrastructure, thus doing much to halt the North's assault on South Vietnam. It was perhaps no coincidence that within six months of the resumption of the bombing, the Hanoi government had indicated its interest in peace talks. On 23 October 1972 Nixon, in return, suspended American strikes north of the 20th parallel.

This suspension did not last long. The peace talks broke down yet again, whereupon Nixon decided to unleash the full force of his air power against North Vietnam, using not only tactical strike aircraft but also, for the first time over Hanoi and Haiphong, the mighty B-52 Stratofortress strategic bomber. On 18 December, the Americans launched Operation Linebacker II, which continued until 30 December. The results of this 11-day offensive (no attacks were mounted on Christmas Day) were, from Nixon's point of view, extremely satisfying. For the loss of only 26 aircraft (15 of them B-52s), the United States managed to smash North Vietnam's extensive air defenses and to destroy most targets of military significance in the Hanoi-Haiphong area. The Linebacker raids did not lead to any fundamental revision of the terms of settlement, but they did induce the North Vietnamese to return to the conference table and to agree, on 23 January 1973, to a ceasefire.

Republic F-105D Thunderchief
Type: Single-seat tactical strike aircraft.
Performance: Max speed 2235km/h (1390mph) at 11,000m. (36,000ft) and 1375km/h (855mph) at sea level.
Service ceiling 15,250m (50,000ft).
Range 3846km (2390 miles).
Armament: One 20mm (0.8in) M-61 cannon with 1029 rounds, plus up to 5450kg (12,000lb) of ordnance, including 'iron' bombs, rockets, AGM-12 Bullpup air-to-surface and AIM-9 Sidewinder air-to-air missiles.

Boeing B-52D Stratofortress
Type: Long-range strategic bomber.
Performance: Max speed 1014km/h (630mph) at over 7315m (24,000ft).
Service ceiling 13,720-16,765m (45,000-55,000ft).
Range on internal fuel with max load 9978km (6200 miles).
Armament: Four 12.7mm (0.5in) M-3 guns; up to 31,750kg (70,000lb) of 'iron' bombs.

McDonnell-Douglas F-4E Phantom II
Type: Two-seat multirole fighter bomber.
Performance: Max speed 2304km/h (1430mph).
Service ceiling 17,907m (58,750ft).
Range 2817km (1750 miles).
Armament: One 20mm (0.8in) M-61-A1 cannon plus up to 7258kg (16,000lb) of ordnance in various combinations; four Sparrow and four Sidewinder air-to-air missiles.

RIGHT: *A cutaway drawing of a Dassault-Breguet Mirage 2000 multirole fighter, capable of undertaking a low-level bombing role. Produced in the late 1970s, the 2000 enjoys a top speed of Mach 2.35 or 2495km/h (1550mph) and an armament fit which includes two 30mm DEFA cannon and up to 5000kg (11,000lb) of bombs and missiles.*

ABOVE: *An interior view of the cockpit of a Boeing B-52 Stratofortress: the pilot is seated on the left.*
LEFT: *A Tupolev Tu-95 strategic bomber (NATO codename 'Bear-D'), photographed while on a reconnaissance flight over the North Atlantic. The first versions of the Bear appeared as early as 1955 and the aircraft is still in service today.*

RECONNAISSANCE

LEFT: *The pilot's view from a North American OV-10A Bronco COIN and night surveillance aircraft of the USAF, showing the excellent visibility enjoyed. OV-10s were used in Vietnam for locating and identifying ground targets.*

RIGHT: *A McDonnell-Douglas F-4B Phantom II of the US Navy's Fighter Squadron VF-21 from the carrier USS Midway drops part of its load of 7257kg (16,000lb) of bombs onto a target in Vietnam, 1965.*

BELOW: *The menacing, almost 'science-fiction' shape of the Lockheed SR-71A Blackbird. All SR-71s serve with the 9th Strategic Reconnaissance Wing at Beale AFB, California, but examples fly regularly from forward operating bases at Kadena in Okinawa and Mildenhall in the UK. Each aircraft has the ability to survey 260,000 sq km (100,000 sq miles) of the earth's surface in one hour.*

FAR LEFT: *The ill-fated British Aerospace Nimrod AEW Mark 3 AWACS (airborne warning and control system). Ordered by the British in preference to the American Boeing E3-A, the Nimrod was to incorporate Marconi pulsed-Doppler surveillance radar, but the project was canceled in 1987.*

ABOVE: *The Boeing E-3A AWACS in USAF colors, Introduced in 1977, the AWACS is designed to monitor enemy air movements, utilizing the Doppler radar housed in its radome.*

LEFT: *A Westland Sea King helicopter, converted to an airborne early warning role by the addition of Thorn-EMI Searchwater radar in a 'kettledrum' on the side.*

of taking accurate photographs from a height of 16,800m (55,000ft) – so accurate, apparently, that enlargements would reveal objects the size of golf balls on a putting green. It also carried ECM equipment that could detect most of the radio and radar signals being transmitted from the territory below.

Originally ordered for and funded by America's Central Intelligence Agency (CIA), the U-2 had been developed in conditions of great secrecy, the designation U (for utility) being an attempt to disguise the aircraft's real purpose. In fact by the time the USAF received its first U-2s a number of these aircraft were already being operated by the CIA, although their ostensible user was the National Aeronautical and Space Administration (NASA). In July 1956 the CIA began sending (unmarked) U-2s over the ·Soviet Union, at first apparently from bases in West Germany and England, later from bases in such countries as Turkey and Japan.

These missions were highly successful until Powers' plane was brought down over Sverdlovsk.

This setback led to a reduction in over-flights of Soviet Asia, but the Americans (principally hereafter the USAF rather than the CIA) continued to make considerable use of U-2s elsewhere, notably over Cuba. Indeed, after the loss of many of their agents in Cuba in the spring and summer of 1961, the Americans fell back upon the U-2 as their principal means of gathering intelligence from the island, and these aircraft subsequently played a key part in monitoring the build-up of Soviet surface-to-air missile (SAM) sites and nuclear-missile installations on the island, a build-up that climaxed in the Cuban missile crisis of October 1962. One U-2 was lost (to a SAM) during the period of the crisis but U-2 overflights provided the American government with invaluable information both before and during the crisis. Shortly after this, in 1964, the

United States deployed U-2s to Southeast Asia, where they were used to provide information necessary to select targets for the bombing of North Vietnam. The Americans (and the Nationalist Chinese) also continued to conduct U-2 flights over mainland China, although by the mid-1970s, after at least eight U-2s had been lost, such operations were reportedly discontinued.

Recognizing that the U-2 was becoming increasingly vulner-

able, the Americans had in the meantime developed a strategic reconnaissance aircraft capable of flying higher and much faster. This successor to the U-2 was the Lockheed SR-71 Blackbird, which is reputed to be able to fly at over Mach 3, at altitudes above 25,900m (85,000ft) and over ranges of 4800km (2982 miles). Like the U-2, the Blackbird was developed in conditions of the utmost secrecy, with much of the funding coming from the CIA, reflected

RIGHT: *A cutaway drawing of a Grumman E-2C Hawkeye airborne early warning and control platform of VAW-125, deployed on board the carrier USS* John F Kennedy. *First flown in prototype form in April 1960, the first examples of the Hawkeye were embarked aboard the carrier USS* Kitty Hawk *in October 1965, but the E-2C variant did not appear in front-line service until 1974. Current examples are fitted with General Electric APS-125 search radar and a variety of other sensors, giving the aircraft the ability to track more than 250 possible targets simultaneously while guiding up to 30 airborne interceptors toward them. A number of E-2Cs have been provided to the Israelis, where they have been fitted with locally produced electronic equipment.*

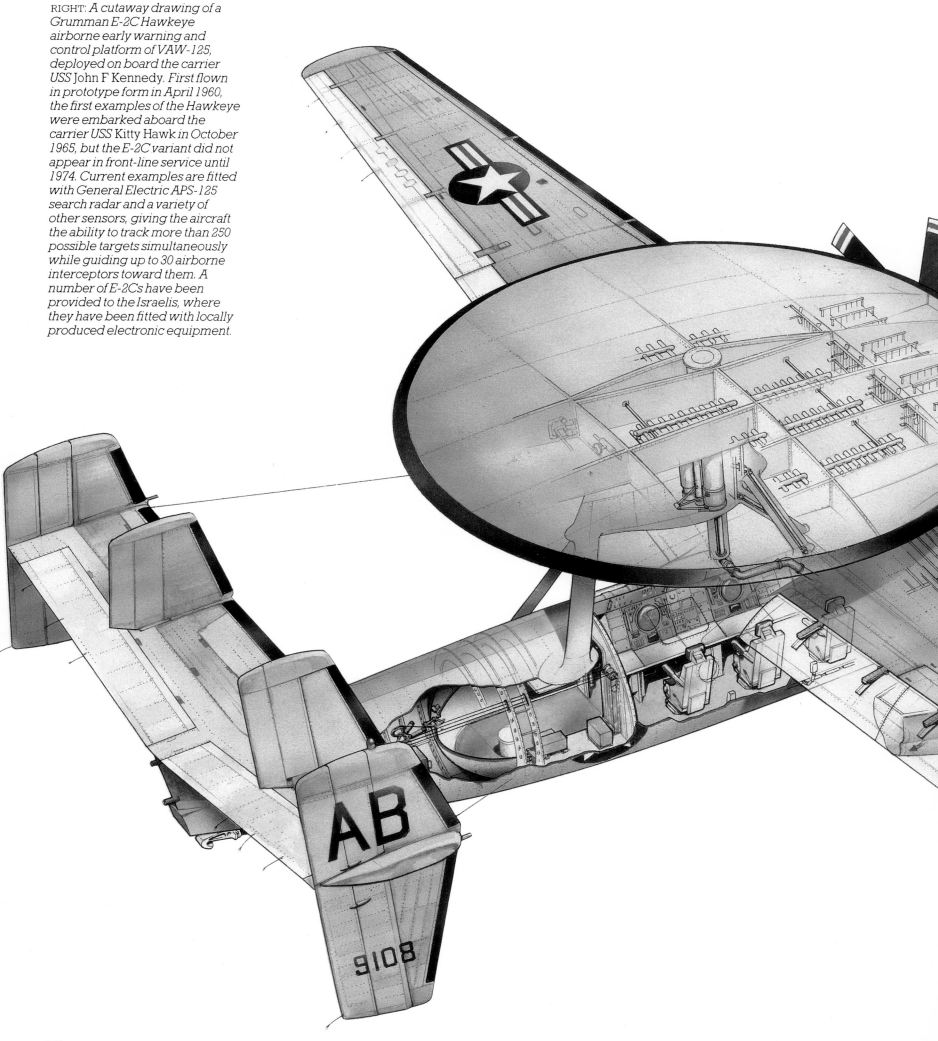

TOP: *An E-2A Hawkeye, having been brought up from the hangar deck with wings folded, is prepared for operation on board the carrier USS Constellation, August 1966. Although outwardly identical to the E-2C, this earlier version was fitted with less sophisticated surveillance devices.* ABOVE: *A Grumman OV-1B Mohawk two-seat battlefield surveillance/ reconnaissance aircraft, fitted with AN/APS-94 equipment in an SLAR (side-looking airborne radar) pod.*

in the fact that in its original version the Blackbird carried the designation A-12 (the first examples to appear were CIA 'company' possessions). The first such aircraft revealed publicly were A-12s modified for evaluation in the interceptor role, bearing the designation YF-12A, three examples of which were displayed at Edwards Air Force Base in September 1964. Shortly afterward, however, the A-12 entered service with the United States Air Force in the form of a strategic reconnaissance aircraft, and bearing the designation SR-71A.

The exact details of the Blackbird's operational history remain shrouded in secrecy, but the SR-71A is believed to have operated over Vietnam, China, the Middle East and Cuba, to name but a few troublespots. Whatever the true extent of its operations, the Blackbird is certainly in a league apart from other combat aircraft, being constructed largely of titanium alloys (so as to resist extremely high temperatures at high speed), powered by a turbojet/ramjet hybrid powerplant, and capable of attaining speeds and altitudes that render it almost futuristic.

TRANSPORT

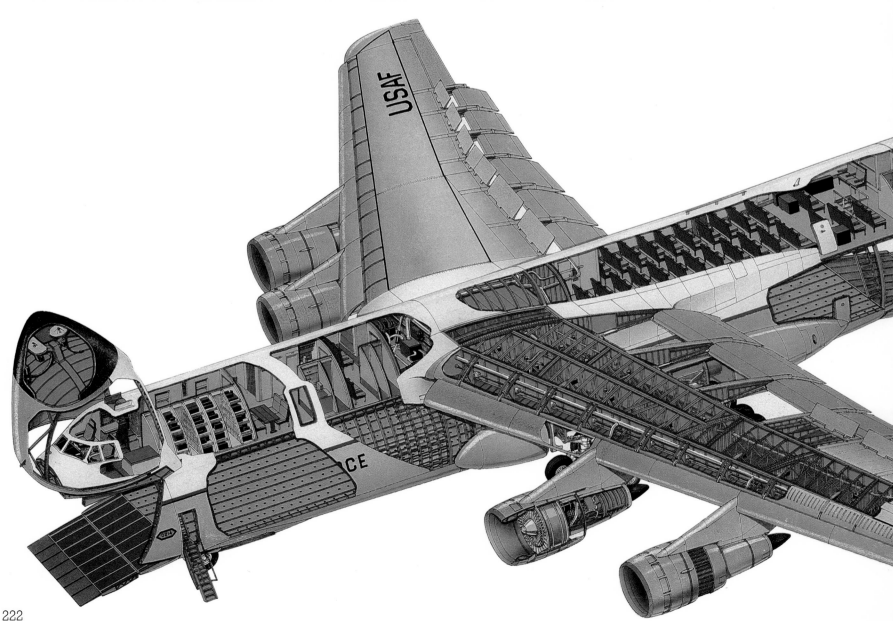

Air Transport
The Lockheed C-130 Hercules

Over the last 30 years, the Lockheed C-130 Hercules has become what the Douglas C-47/53 Dakota was to the wartime United States and her allies: the ubiquitous workhorse of the skies. One of the first wholly postwar transports, the Hercules has probably proved the most successful, finding employment in over 40 variants and in the service of 57 nations. Though dwarfed by Lockheed's two later transports, the C-141 Starlifter and the C-5 Galaxy, the Hercules remains probably the most versatile transport in service in the world at the present time.

The specification that was to lead to the Hercules was laid down by the USAF as early as 1951, just two years after the start of service deliveries of its immediate predecessor, the Fairchild C-119 Boxcar. The latter, however, was distinctly World War II vintage, and indeed it first flew in 1944. The Hercules, on the other hand, was unmistakably postwar in that its distinctive silhouette and four turboprop engines set it apart from earlier transports, although in reality the newcomer, in technological terms, was not innovative. For the most part the Hercules incorporated tried and tested technology, but did so in such an effective manner that subsequent in-service development, advanced through four major production serials, has resulted in improved carrying capacity with no loss in terms of range and speed.

The Hercules was designed and built around the standard US railroad boxcar, or, more accurately, around a cargo hold large enough to take the 12m × 3m × 2.7m (40ft × 10ft × 9ft) boxcar. Ease of loading dictated that the floor of the hold should be 1143mm (45in) above the ground, the same clearance as the standard American truck, and these two requirements in turn predicated three of the distinctive features of the Hercules: first, a high cantilevered wing that allowed the aircraft's fuselage to sit close to the ground; second, the incorporation of the main undercarriage

TOP LEFT: *Head-on view of the formidable Lockheed C-5 Galaxy strategic logistical transport aircraft. First flown on 20 June 1968, the Galaxy began to enter service with the US Military Airlift Command in December 1969.*
LEFT: *A cutaway drawing of a C-5 Galaxy transport, giving some idea of its enormous lift capability. Each C-5 can carry up to 100,228kg (220,967lb) of general cargo or 350 fully armed troops with their immediate equipment.*
BELOW: *A striking photograph of Canadian C-130 Hercules transports.*

ABOVE: *A Hercules transport in US service uses its renowned short take-off ability to lift away from an airstrip, while another waits its turn, engines revving.*
FAR LEFT, TOP: *An artist's impression of the USAF's new transport aircraft, the C-17.*
FAR LEFT, BELOW: *A Lockheed C-130E transport aircraft carries out a familiar role, dropping supplies by parachute from its rear cargo door, in a 1974 exercise.*
LEFT: *Britain's RAF has recently acquired six Tristar aircraft for conversion to the tanker/transport role.*

within fairings mounted in the lower fuselage, the width of the aircraft ensuring stability on the part of the two main wheels mounted in tandem on either side; third, the abruptly upswept rear fuselage with its two-section rear door, the lower section of which acted as the loading ramp. With a fully pressurized compartment, a wholly cylindrical hold as far back as the rear fuselage, four engines and an enormous tail unit with large controls to ensure good handling characteristics at low speeds, the Hercules first flew in August 1954. Trials quickly revealed that in terms of maximum speed 588km/h (365mph), range 4022km (2500 miles) and payload 18,160kg (40,000lb), the Hercules exceeded design requirements and was at least the equal of any radial-powered transport then in service. Moreover, these trials showed two characteristics that made it far superior to its predecessors and contemporaries. First, even without jet-assisted take-off, the Hercules could become airborne inside 274m (900ft) and land in 183m (600ft) with a 7264kg (16,000lb) load, and it was able to operate from ill-prepared bases and even from ice and snow. Second, the Hercules could carry a number of loads and could be converted between loads in very short order. Capable of carrying 18,160kg (40,000lb) of cargo, 72 troops or 70 stretcher cases (plus six medical personnel), the

ABOVE: *In addition to its designated role as a transport, the C-130 has also proved useful for in-flight refueling duties, as shown in this photograph of two US Marine Corps F-4 Phantom IIs linked up to a Hercules.*

Hercules could be converted from a troop carrier to airlanding cargo carrier in 20 minutes or to the heavy-drop role in 40. After entering service in December 1956, the Hercules proved the success that had been anticipated, the first production orders having been placed before the first prototype flew.

In service, the great flexibility of the Hercules allowed its employment in a number of roles, some hardly befitting so dignified an aircraft as a transport. In Vietnam the Hercules was employed as a heavily armed gunship, for night surveillance, fire control and electronic countermeasures (ECM) duties, and on covert operations. In the latter role the Hercules was often employed on exfiltration of personnel, using recovery techniques that had been developed as part of the American space program. It was also pressed into service as a tanker for both fixed-wing aircraft and helicopters, and saw service as a search and rescue/maritime patrol aircraft and as a communications relay center for patrol submarines. But important though these and other roles have been, the Hercules remains primarily a medium transport, capable of operating anywhere in the world with a good payload. It was in this role, of course, that the Hercules figured prominently in relief

operations in Ethiopia in the mid-1980s, the aircraft's ability to drop palletized 11,350kg (25,000lb) loads from very low altitude being crucial to what success was commanded in that effort – although its actions in other relief operations, such as those in Nepal in 1973, should not be forgotten. Its ability to operate from virtually any kind of surface at altitudes between sea level and the foothills of the Himalayas, in extremes of climate, and with a variety of loads has ensured that production continues, 33 years after it began, at a rate of three aircraft a month. To date more than 1750 military and 100 civil C-130 Hercules have been built, of which 700 of the military version have been for export. In service with 14 squadrons, the bulk of the USAF's tactical airlift strength, the Hercules is certain to remain the mainstay of the American transport service for many years to come, although with the development of the C-17 replacement program belatedly in progress, future C-130 production is certain to be directed to foreign buyers.

Lockheed C-130H

Type: Multirole airlift transport
Performance: Max speed 588km/h (365mph).
Service ceiling 8075m (26,500ft).
Range 4022km (2500 miles).
Armament: None normally carried.

RIGHT: *A Fairchild AC-119 Shadow gunship, armed with 7.62mm machine-guns, flies over the coast of South Vietnam, searching for ground targets. The Shadow was a 1960s' conversion of the C-119 Flying Boxcar tactical transport aircraft, a design which had its origins in World War II. Throughout the 1950s and into the 1960s, the Flying Boxcar was a familiar sight in conflicts as far apart as Indochina, the Belgian Congo, Korea and Vietnam.*

BELOW: *Soviet paratroopers wait to emplane in an Ilyushin Il-76 strategic/tactical transport aircraft (NATO codename 'Candid'). Introduced in March 1971, the Il-76 is one of the best aircraft in the world at dealing with rough airstrips. It can carry up to 35,000kg (77,160lb) of cargo over a range of 6400km (3975 miles) or, as the photograph implies, a 'stick' of 140 paratroops. The manned tail turret, with 23mm cannon, may be seen.*

NAVAL AVIATION

Naval Aviation
The Hawker Siddeley/British Aerospace Sea Harrier

Nearly 30 years after it first took to the air, the Harrier remains the only vertical/short take-off and landing (V/STOL) jet aircraft in operational service in the world. Until proven in combat in the South Atlantic in 1982 it remained something of a curiosity, technically impressive but perhaps an appropriate epitaph for a British aviation industry whose last solely national product it was – though it must be noted that the final stages of the development program were ensured only by American funding.

The Harrier originated in the late 1950s in the realization that the unprecedented power-to-weight ratios conferred by jet engines made vertical take-off and landing (VTOL) possible. For aircraft operating in the close-support role, VTOL presented a number of obvious advantages, the most important being use from pre-selected dispersed sites away from airfields that were certain to be priority targets in the event of war – as proved in the 1967 Arab-Israeli War. Able to operate from roads, leveled fields and even urban centers immediately behind the front-line, a VTOL aircraft, because of its ability to respond quickly over short distances to demands on its services, obviated the need for a 'cab rank' of more sophisticated conventional aircraft over the battlefield. VTOL, however, was not without its drawbacks, most notably the relatively low performance of such aircraft, the large support element

needed to maintain dispersed units, and the vulnerability of forward sites to changes in the tactical situation on the ground. Nevertheless, it was to be in the close-support role that the Harrier entered service with the Royal Air Force (RAF) in April 1969.

More than eight years elapsed between the Harrier's first taking to the air (21 October 1960) and its entering service and this was the result of three factors: traditional prejudice against so revolutionary an aircraft; its lengthy development program; and the confusion caused by conflicting requirements that reflected an uncertain British procurement policy in the 1960s. Indeed, despite the Harrier's first fully successful transition from vertical take-off (VTO) to forward flight on 22 September 1961, its first short take-off (STO) in October 1961 and its trinational evaluation after January

LEFT: *A British Aerospace Sea Harrier FRS Mark I single-seat V/STOL (vertical/short take-off and landing) multirole combat aircraft uses the specially designed 'ski-jump' at the end of a carrier deck to achieve extra lift. The advantage of this is that fuel spent on vertical take-off is saved.*
BELOW: *The aircraft carrier USS* Coral Sea *under way near the Philippines in 1982. Among the aircraft on the ship's deck are F-4 Phantoms and A-6 Intruders. The* Coral Sea, *which was commissioned in 1947, is powered by steam turbines. Because of her relatively small size she has to operate reduced air groups of F-4s.*

RIGHT: *Four Yakovlev Yak-36MP single-seat light VTOL (vertical take-off and landing) shipborne strike fighters (NATO codename 'Forger') line the flightdeck of Soviet cruiser-carrier* Kiev, *November 1982.*

FAR RIGHT, TOP: *Vought A-7 Corsair II single-seat close support and interdiction aircraft of the USAF, photographed in 1980. A-7s achieved impressive bombing accuracy in Vietnam.*

FAR RIGHT, BELOW: *A Grumman F-14A Tomcat two-seat, carrier-borne multirole combat aircraft. A potent warplane, the F-14A has a top speed of Mach 2.34 or 2517km/h (1564mph) and a weapons fit which includes the impressive AIM-54 Phoenix missile, linked to the AN/AWG-9 control system, capable of tracking 24 targets simultaneously and attacking six of the more dangerous.*

BELOW: *A Kamov Ka-27 helicopter (NATO codename 'Helix') aboard the Soviet guided missile destroyer* Udaloy *in 1981. The Helix is the most modern Soviet naval helicopter and is believed to have antisubmarine and missile targeting capabilities.*

1964, it was not until the cancellation of the TSR-2, AW-631 and, crucially, the P-1154 Mach 2 VTOL programs in February 1965 that the Harrier's future was assured. It was only when rival programs were scrapped that Harrier development and production proceeded, although by 1965 most of the more serious shortcomings of the VTOL concept were well on the way to being eliminated. The most crucial of these was the fact that the first Harriers lacked range and an effective payload: indeed the first flight was made by a stripped Harrier that could do little more than lift itself off the ground. A series of improvements to engine performance in the 1960s ultimately paved the way for the Rolls-Royce Pegasus 103 engine that, in the GR3 version, developed 9761kg (21,500lb) thrust and gave the Harrier a very respectable performance: an ability to take off inside 396m (1300ft) and to carry either a 1135kg (2500lb) load to 96.5km (60 miles) range from a VTO or a 2270kg (5,000lb) load to a range of 274km (170 miles) from 610m (2,000ft) STO.

Although the Harrier was British and conceived for an RAF requirement, the tactical flexibility conferred by VTOL immediately attracted American and naval attention. In the 1950s and early 1960s naval VTOL was seen as a supplement to conventional carrier aviation, but after 1966 the Royal Navy, faced with the phasing from service of its remaining carriers, turned to the Harrier as the only means by which it could retain a fixed-wing capability at sea. As a result the Sea Harrier, a fully navalized version of the GR3 but with superior avionics, was ordered in 1975 for the three 'Invincible' class ships, the name-ship entering service in 1978 after having been ordered in 1972. The Royal Navy proved fortunate in that the aircraft's performance was to be effectively doubled in terms of load or range by the development of the ski-ramp between 1972 and 1977. In order to accommodate their Sea Dart system, the *Invincible* and *Illustrious* were fitted with seven-degree ramps, the later *Ark Royal* and older *Hermes*, with ramps set at 12 degrees.

LEFT: *Soviet helicopter carriers and cruisers deploy the Kamov Ka-25 'Hormone' in the antisubmarine role.*

BELOW RIGHT: *The first prototype Harrier GR.5 goes on display. The GR.5 is the new version of the Harrier, similar to the US Marines' AV-8B, which is to enter service with the RAF in the late 1980s.*

BOTTOM RIGHT: *A Super Etendard of the French Navy with an Exocet antiship missile.*

BELOW: *An A-6E Intruder attack aircraft of Attack Squadron 65 of the US Navy.*

BOTTOM: *Harriers of the US Marines. The Marines value the Harrier's ability to support a landing operation from quickly improvised airfields.*

Thus equipped, it was the *Invincible* and *Hermes*, with their Sea Harriers, that were the difference between defeat and victory in the South Atlantic in 1982. The 28 Sea Harriers operated by the ships accounted for 20 of the total 102 aircraft lost by Argentina and along with 14 RAF Harrier GR3s, supported operations ashore. Overall, they lost 10 of their number but none in aerial combat. The aircraft's ability to decelerate rapidly by adjusting its engines enabled it to out-maneuver such technically superior aircraft as the Dagger or Mirage, the vectoring of engines by a Harrier forcing a pursuer to overshoot its intended victim and thus present itself as a target for the Harrier's guns and Sidewinder missiles. The 1982 demonstration of its suspected abilities as an interceptor, however, brought no fresh orders. The Sea Harrier is still in service with only the British, Indian and Spanish navies.

The largest single employer of the Harrier remains the US Marine Corps, which placed orders in 1969 and took delivery of the redesignated AV-8A during and after 1971. For a service committed to assault landings and fighting from a beachhead, the Harrier represented an effective combination of aircraft performance and helicopter-type lift. Marine Corps requirements, however, have ensured American preponderance in subsequent research and development, this being recognized by Britain in 1979 in her acceptance that the next-generation AV-8B Harrier II/RAF Harrier GR5 should be developed around American criteria and the existing AV-8A aircraft. The fact remains, however, that while the new Harrier will be a considerable technical improvement over its predecessor in terms of engine-life, power of maneuver, range and all-round visibility, its very limited improvement of performance in terms of speed and payload is unlikely to create much interest beyond the ranks of those who already operate its existing version.

British Aerospace Sea Harrier FRS1
Type: Single-seat carrier-borne V/STOL fighter.
Performance: Max speed 1187km/h (737mph).
Service ceiling 16,760m (55,000ft).
Range in combat 667km (414 miles).
Armament: Two fixed 30mm (1.2in) cannon; up to 2270kg (5000lb) of stores on four wing hardpoints and fuselage centerline, including Sidewinder air-to-air missiles, bombs or rockets.

FUTURE TRENDS

Future Trends
Aircraft and New Technology

Modern war can be a complex business, dependent to a very large extent upon technology. In the immediate future, as the pace of technological change is accelerated, a number of trends should become apparent. Enhanced electronic aids should enable enemy movements to be monitored more accurately and at a greater distance, while improved guidance and tracking systems should allow targets to be destroyed with almost guaranteed success. At the same time, weapons delivery platforms, whether on land, at sea or in the air, should be able to survive the attentions of the enemy, either through increased mobility or less obvious radar, infrared or electronic 'signatures.' Such changes will clearly affect defenders just as much as aggressors, so a rough balance will probably ensue, but the pendulum of advantage between attack and defense is likely to swing so rapidly that an accurate assessment of its position at any particular moment in time will become increasingly difficult to make.

Aircraft are affected by technology to a greater extent than land or even naval systems, partly because they are, in themselves, the products of technology, but also because air warfare, with its three-dimensional framework, requires technological aids to be effective. The first priority is survivability, for it would not be much use having aircraft which were so vulnerable to enemy radars and antiair defenses that they were shot down the moment they approached enemy territory. In the past, speed and altitude were the main features of survival, but with improved surface-to-air missiles (SAMs) firing heat or electronic seeking munitions, this is not so applicable today. As both the Americans in Vietnam (1972) and the Israelis over the Beqa'a Valley (1982) showed, it may be possible to solve the problem by devising an elaborate 'package' of offensive air power, committing specially equipped electronic-warfare aircraft first, to monitor and jam enemy radars, followed by other machines dedicated to SAM suppression, but this is expensive and, as SAMs become less dependent upon 'active' radar for target location, it is less likely to succeed. The only answer seems to lie in 'stealth' technology which makes the aircraft itself less susceptible to electronic or radar interception, enabling it to penetrate enemy airspace without triggering defensive systems.

The basic idea is to make the aircraft 'invisible' to enemy radars and electronic systems, and a number of technological avenues are currently being explored. Most existing aircraft, with their bulky fuselages and large jet engines, produce a substantial radar cross-section – the B-52 Stratofortress bomber, for example, has radar-reflective surfaces equal to 100sq m (1080sq ft), making it easy to track – but if special attention is paid to contour control, producing rounded lines and wing-body blending, this can be reduced quite dramatically. The Rockwell B-1 bomber, for example, has molded wing-edges, blended configuration and a thin cross-section, producing a radar signature, in the B-1B, of less than 1sq m (11sq ft). At the same time, engine outlets can be 'hidden' to reduce heat signature, and certain parts of the body of the

BELOW LEFT: *The prototype of Israel's Lavi jet fighter, presented to the world on 21 July 1986. The Lavi was meant to be the first combat aircraft to be manufactured entirely in Israel, with a production run of 300, but costs have escalated and the future looks bleak. Each fighter will eventually cost a staggering $24 million.*
LEFT: *A Boeing AGM-86B ALCM (air-launched cruise missile) emerges from the bomb-bay of a B-52G heavy bomber during flight trials over California.*

aircraft can be manufactured from radar-absorbent material, designed to absorb or deflect radar waves. Finally, as aircraft can be tracked by means of their infrared or electronic emissions, experiments have been conducted in the reduction of engine heat (something which suggests a future trend away from supersonic flight, which produces a high heat signature) and the development of 'passive' navigation or bomb-aiming aids which, by depending on inertial systems, will not emit signals which the enemy would be able to monitor.

Serious work on stealth technology probably began in the United States in the late 1970s, under conditions of strict security, centered upon the XST (Experimental Stealth Tactical) fighter, produced by Lockheed. First flown in 1977 and ordered into production four years later (as the F-19), it is generally believed that at least a squadron of these aircraft currently exists, possibly at Nellis Air Force Base in California. Comprising a large, rounded fuselage with a relatively small wing, the F-19 is reported to look rather like the Space Shuttle. Crashes have occurred – the most recent in 1986 – but security is maintained, even to the extent of throwing a military cordon around the crash site. Similar security surrounds the other known area of research, carried out by Northrop under the designation ATB (Advanced Technology Bomber). Details of this are understandably sparse, but the ATB is widely believed to comprise a very futuristic 'flying wing' design, in which fuselage and wing are closely blended to produce a 'flat' arrow shape, with air intakes and engine exhausts concealed and all vertical surfaces deleted. If this is true, the shape of aircraft in the future will change dramatically.

But stealth technology is only one area of potential change, for aircraft have roles other than airspace penetration to perform. Chief among these, at a tactical level, is to act as platforms for target-location devices and, again, the Americans lead the field in developing appropriate technology. The huge Boeing A-3 Sentry AWACS (Airborne Warning and Control System), with its distinctive radome mounted above the fuselage, is the most familiar of these aircraft, and has been in service with the USAF since 1977, but this is only one aspect of current development. Joint-STARS (Joint Surveillance and Target Attack Radar System), for example, uses a C-18 adaptation of the Boeing 707 to monitor enemy radar emissions, collating the information through on-board computers and passing it on to ground-based artillery units. Even more sophisticated is PLSS (Precision Location Strike System), in which Lockheed TR-1 aircraft (modernized examples of the U-2 'spy-plane') will operate in threes, flying in pre-set 'race-track' patterns which will enable enemy emissions to be located with precision by means of triangulation, the information once again being transmitted to strike forces, this time in the air. PLSS, however, has run into funding difficulties and may not appear in its projected form.

Once targets have been located, they will be attacked using new generations of weapons, based on 'stand-off' systems which do not entail the penetration of enemy airspace by expensive aircraft. The ALCM (Air Launched Cruise Missile) is one such system, being able to glide from high launch altitude to its operating level of 15m (50ft) above the ground, after which it follows a pre-set course with corrections being made via the revolutionary TER-COM (TERrain Contour Matching Guidance) system mounted on board. The idea is that, if the TERCOM computer finds that the ALCM is flying over terrain which does not match its pre-set 'memory' (itself dependent upon satellite photographs of the chosen route), it will fire the engine to make flight corrections. This means that a very indirect route can be taken and that high accuracy – reckoned to be 18.3m (60ft) over a range of 2780km (1725 miles) – is virtually guaranteed, even with a conventional (non-nuclear) warhead. At shorter ranges, glide bombs (with no on-course correction facility) such as the GBU-15, can be employed.

But if the intention of such technology is to avoid pilot or aircraft loss, other options do exist. The most obvious is to develop and deploy RPVs (Remotely Piloted Vehicles) which, because of their low unit cost, are much more expendable. RPVs first appeared in the late 1960s, being used by the Americans to monitor emissions

from special electronic listening devices spread across likely Viet Cong infiltration routes in Vietnam, but more sophisticated examples now exist. During the Israeli invasion of southern Lebanon in June 1982, for example, RPVs were used not only to 'trigger' Syrian SAM radars in the Beqa'a Valley – providing the Israeli Air Force with precise wavelengths for electronic countermeasures (ECM) pods on board attacking aircraft, capable of jamming the radar sets – but also to provide 'real-time' information to commanders in the field by mounting television cameras on board. Since then, moreover, further experiments have provided RPVs with their own strike capability, usually laser- or TV-guided missiles which will be able to take out a designated target with great accuracy. A new generation of 'fire-and-forget' missiles, with their own target-seekers on board, should improve the potential yet more.

If this is the way of the future, we are on the brink of a new era of air warfare, based upon stealth and automation. The shape, capabilities and survivability of aircraft seem set to change quite dramatically in the next few years, although it is worth noting that none of this will alter the basic roles to be carried out in future war. Bombing, ground-attack, interdiction, interception, maintenance of airspace, naval support, transportation, reconnaissance and observation all remain as important today as they were in 1918 or 1945 and are likely to be so for years to come.

ABOVE LEFT: *An artist's impression of the British Aerospace EAP (experimental aircraft program) – part of the work for the EFA (European fighter aircraft). The EAP flew in August 1986.*

LEFT: *A Lockheed TR-1 tactical reconnaissance aircraft in flight. Basically an updated version of the U-2, the TR-1 is designed to carry the UPD-X side-looking airborne radar and to play an integral part in the Lockheed PLSS (Precision Location Strike System).*

BELOW: *An American Pioneer RPV (Remotely Piloted Vehicle) is boosted from the deck of the battleship USS Iowa during recent trials. The RPV has the ability to provide reconnaissance information out to a range of 177km (110 miles) before being recovered.*

237

INDEX

Acknowledgments

We would like to thank David Copsey who designed this book; Andrea Stern, the picture researcher; Wendy Sacks, the editor; and Ron Watson, the indexer. Our thanks, too, to all those who supplied illustrations on the pages listed, and to Tony Bryan and Peter Sarson for producing the cutaway illustrations.

Alexander Aviation: pages 38-39 (below)
Aviation Photographs International: pages 7 (top left), 20 (both), 21, 24 (top), 32 (left), 120 (top), 144 (top), 145 (below), 236-7 (below)
Aviation Picture Library/Austin Brown: pages 11 (top), 77 (below), 113 (below), 132, 149 (below), 161 (top), 193 (below)
Aviation Picture Library/Mark Wagner: page 171
BBC Hulton Picture Library: pages 43 (top), 47 (top), 54 (below), 73 (top), 102 (top)
BBC Hulton/Bettmann Archive: pages 57 (top), 59 (below)
Bison Picture Library: pages 1, 37 (below), 60-61 (below), 82-3 (all pictures), 84 (top & center left), 86 (below), 86-7 (below), 89 (top), 90 (top), 93 (center), 100 (below), 110 (below left), 111 (top), 112 (top), 114 (top), 124 (below), 125 (top), 131 (top), 138-9, 142 (top), 153 (below), 158 (top), 168, 176 (below), 178 (top), 181 (top), 182, 191 (top), 194, 195 (top), 202, 203 (top), 205 (both

pictures), 210 (below), 211 (below left & right), 221 (below), 223 (below), 227 (top)
Chaz Bowyer: pages 14, 22, 30-31, 49 (top), 60 (top right), 84-5, 111 (below), 122, 126 (below), 127 (below)
British Aerospace: pages 95 (top), 164-5, 168, 192, 228, 232 (below), 233 (top), 236-7 (top)
Camera Press: pages 35 (top right), 51 (top), 95 (below)
Phil Chinnery: pages 186-7 (both)
Department of Defense (USA): page 224 (below)
Roger Freeman: pages 78-9 (below), 170
M J Hooks: pages 4-5, 6, 15 (below), 17 (top), 25 (center right), 26-7 (below), 37 (top), 39 (top), 40 (below), 43 (below), 58 (below), 61 (top), 70 (top), 70-1 (below), 77 (top), 78-9 (top), 85 (top), 98-9 (below), 101 (below), 105 (top), 109 (top), 112 (below), 113 (top), 115 (top), 118 (top), 124 (top), 125 (below), 130-1 (below), 161 (below), 184 (top), 224 (top), 233 (below)
Robert Hunt Library: pages 12 (below), 23 (top), 38 (top), 42 (both), 45 (top), 46 (below), 48 (both), 49 (below), 50-1, 54-5 (top), 68-9, 81 (top), 88, 108-9, 123 (top), 126 (top), 128 (top), 139 (top left), 141 (below), 147 (top), 157 (below), 166
Imperial War Museum, London: pages 13 (below), 17 (below) 19, 23 (below), 27, 28-9, 31 (top), 34 (below), 44 (top), 47 (below), 51 (center right), 52, 53 (both), 55 (below), 58 (top left), 62 (left),

62-3 (below), 63 (top), 64 (top), 65 (both pictures), 66 (both), 67 (both), 72 (top), 76, 91 (center), 93 (top), 96 (top), 101 (top), 109 (center), 119 (center & below), 121 (top), 127 (top), 142 (below), 145 (top), 151 (top), 152-3 (below), 154, 155 (top), 156
Israeli Government Press Office: pages 188-9 (all pictures), 190 (top), 190-1 (below)
Dwight Lee/Warren Thompson: page 173 (top)
Lockheed: page 226
MARS: pages 41, 72 (below), 114 (below), 134 (top)
George McKay/Warren Thompson: page 80 (below)
Ministry of Defence (UK): pages 16 (below), 179 (top), 201 (top), 212 (top), 225 (below)
Peter Newark's Western Americana: pages 11 (below), 12 (top), 15 (top), 60 (top left), 106 (top), 144 (below), 157 (top), 207, 216 (top)
Northrop Corporation: page 179 (below)
Novosti Press Agency: pages 90 (below), 91 (both), 173 (below), 227 (below)
Oscarpix Enterprises: pages 7 (below), 71 (top), 80 (top), 208
Public Archives of Canada: pages 118-19
Quadrant Picture Library, Sutton, Surrey: pages 2-3, 36, 102 (below), 180 (top), 193 (top), 209, 210 (top) 231 (top)
Royal Aeronautical Society: pages 18, 34 (top left), 34-5 (top)
Saab Scania: page 177
Harry Shumate/Warren Thompson: page 7 (top right)

Frank Spooner Pictures: pages 196 (top), 211 (top), 234 (below)
Joe Szabo/Warren Thompson: page 221 (top)
Warren Thompson: page 185 (top)
TPS/Fox Photos: pages 97 (both pictures), 116, 120 (below), 121 (below), 137 (center), 152 (top)
TPS/Three Lions: pages 46 (top), 155 (below)
TRH Pictures: pages 10, 13 (top), 16 (top), 24 (below), 25 (below), 26 (top), 32-3, 40 (center), 44-5 (below), 64 (below), 73 (below), 81 (below), 92-3 (below), 94, 98 (top), 99 (top), 100 (top), 115 (below), 117, 119 (top), 129, 134 (below), 135 (below), 136, 137 (top), 139 (top right), 140 (both), 141 (top), 143, 146, 147 (below), 148-9, 148 (below), 150, 160 (both), 167 (below), 174-5, 176 (top), 187 (below right and center), 197 (both), 199, 200, 201 (below), 208 (top), 213 (top), 214, 215, 216-17 (below), 219 (top), 222, 225 (top), 234-5, 237 (below)
US Air Force: pages 56-7 (below), 58 (top right), 130 (top), 133, 135 (below), 158-9 (below), 167 (top), 172, 183, 185 (bottom right), 206, 217 (top)
US Army: pages 195 (below), 198, 204 (top)
US Navy: pages 59 (below), 175 (top), 178 (below), 229, 230 (both), 231 (below), 232 (top & center)
US Naval Historical Center: page 69 (below)
Westland: page 219 (below)
WZ-Bilddienst: pages 151 (below), 157 (center)